OAHU
TRAVEL GUIDE 2025-2026

Explore North Shore Surfing, Waikīkī Beach, Diamond Head, Pearl Harbor, and Lēʻahi Crater With Full-Color Photos, Maps and Custom Itineraries

Elira Glen

ALL RIGHTS RESERVED

No part of this publication may be reproduced, distributed, or transmitted in any form or by any means, including photocopying, recording, or other electronic or mechanical methods, without the prior written permission of the publisher, except in the case of brief quotations embodied in critical reviews and certain other noncommercial uses permitted by copyright law.

Table of Contents

Chapter 1. Introduction to Oahu — 4
  1.1 Why Visit Oahu? — 4
  1.2 A Brief History of Oahu — 8
  1.3 Oahu's Geography and Climate — 12
  1.4 Best Time to Visit Oahu — 20

Chapter 2. Getting to and Around Oahu — 24
  2.1 Flights to Oahu: International and Domestic Airports — 24
  2.2 Transportation Options: Renting a Car, Public Transit, and Ride-Sharing — 27
  2.3 Navigating the Island: Road Rules and Travel Tips — 30

Chapter 3. Top Attractions in Oahu — 33
  3.1 Pearl Harbor and USS Arizona Memorial — 33
  3.2 Diamond Head State Monument — 36
  3.3 Waikiki Beach and Promenade — 39
  3.4 Hanauma Bay Nature Preserve — 42
  3.5 Iolani Palace — 45
  3.6 Kualoa Ranch & Private Nature Reserve — 48
  3.7 Byodo-In Temple — 51

Chapter 4. Best Beaches in Oahu — 55
  4.1 Lanikai Beach — 55
  4.2 Sunset Beach — 58
  4.3 Kailua Beach Park — 61
  4.4 Waimea Bay — 64
  4.5 Makapu'u Beach — 66
  4.6 Sandy Beach — 68

Chapter 5. Outdoor Adventures and Activities — 71
  5.1 Hiking Trails: Koko Crater, Manoa Falls, and Lanikai Pillbox Trail — 71
  5.2 Snorkeling and Diving Spots: Hanauma Bay and Shark's Cove — 76
  5.3 Surfing: Best Spots for Beginners and Pros — 81

Chapter 6. Where to Stay: Accommodation Options in Oahu — 86
  6.1 Luxury Resorts: Four Seasons Resort Oahu, The Ritz-Carlton Residences Waikiki Beach — 86
  6.2 Mid-Range Hotels: Hilton Hawaiian Village & Moana Surfrider — 89
  6.3 Budget-Friendly Stays in Oahu — 93
  6.4 Vacation Rentals and Boutique Stays in Oahu — 97

Chapter 7. Oahu's Food and Dining Scene — 102
  7.1 Best Local Hawaiian Dishes to Try — 102
  7.2 Top Restaurants in Honolulu — 107
  7.3 Budget-Friendly Eats: Food Trucks and Local Markets — 112
  7.4 Traditional Hawaiian Luaus and Cultural Dining Experiences — 117

Chapter 8. Culture, History, and Local Experiences — 122

    8.1 Polynesian Cultural Center — 122
    8.2 Bishop Museum — 125
    8.3 Historic Downtown Honolulu — 127

Chapter 9. Shopping and Nightlife in Oahu — 130
    9.1 Best Shopping Areas: Ala Moana Center, Waikiki, Local Boutiques — 130
    9.2 Oahu's Nightlife: Beachfront Bars, Clubs, and Live Music Venues — 133
    9.3 Best Spots for Traditional Hawaiian Souvenirs — 136

Chapter 10. Appendices — 140
    10.1 Packing Checklist for Oahu — 141
    10.2 Essential Travel Tips and Local Etiquette — 144
    10.3 Emergency Contacts and Health Services in Oahu — 147
    10.4 Useful Apps and Websites for Travelers in Oahu — 150
    10.5 Recommended Reading and Resources — 153

Chapter 1. Introduction to Oahu

1.1 Why Visit Oahu?

Oahu, often called *The Gathering Place*, is a mesmerizing island where modern city life, breathtaking landscapes, and deep-rooted Hawaiian traditions come together. As the most visited Hawaiian island, Oahu welcomes millions of travelers each year with its world-renowned beaches, historic landmarks, lush mountains, and vibrant culture. Whether you seek adventure, relaxation, history, or local flavors, Oahu offers an unforgettable experience for every type of traveler.

A Perfect Blend of Natural Beauty and Urban Excitement

Oahu is unique because it combines the **buzzing energy of a city with the tranquility of a tropical paradise**. Honolulu, the capital of Hawaii, is a vibrant metropolis filled with skyscrapers, luxury resorts, shopping malls, and a dynamic nightlife scene. Yet, just minutes from the city, you can escape into lush rainforests, hike up volcanic craters, snorkel in turquoise waters, or relax on secluded beaches. This

4

seamless blend of **modern convenience and untouched nature** makes Oahu an ideal destination for those who want a little bit of everything.

World-Famous Beaches and Pristine Waters

Oahu's **stunning beaches are among the best in the world**, each offering a unique experience:

- **Waikiki Beach** – The most famous beach in Hawaii, perfect for beginner surfers, sunbathing, and beachfront dining.
- **Lanikai Beach** – A secluded, powder-white sand beach with clear waters, ideal for kayaking and paddleboarding.
- **Sunset Beach** – A world-class surfing destination, home to massive winter waves and incredible sunsets.
- **Hanauma Bay** – A marine sanctuary where visitors can snorkel with vibrant coral reefs and tropical fish.
- **Waimea Bay** – A picturesque beach known for big wave surfing in winter and calm, crystal-clear waters in summer.
- **Makapu'u Beach** – A dramatic coastline with scenic cliffs and some of the best bodyboarding waves.
- **Ko Olina Lagoons** – A family-friendly resort area with gentle waters, ideal for swimming and relaxation.

Whether you're a **surfer chasing the perfect wave**, a **snorkeler exploring underwater wonders**, or someone who simply wants to **relax on soft golden sand**, Oahu's beaches offer something for everyone.

Rich Hawaiian History and Cultural Experiences

Oahu is the **historical and cultural heart of Hawaii**, with deep connections to the past and a strong commitment to preserving traditions. Visitors can immerse themselves in Hawaiian heritage through **historical landmarks, cultural performances, and museums**.

- **Pearl Harbor & USS Arizona Memorial** – A powerful tribute to the lives lost during the attack on December 7, 1941.
- **Iolani Palace** – The only royal palace in the United States, once home to Hawaii's last monarchs.
- **Bishop Museum** – A fascinating museum showcasing Hawaiian history, artifacts, and ancient traditions.
- **Polynesian Cultural Center** – An immersive experience where visitors can learn about Hawaiian and Pacific Islander cultures.

- **Hawaiian Luaus** – Experience a traditional Hawaiian feast with fire dancers, hula performances, and local delicacies.

From **ancient Hawaiian traditions** to **World War II history**, Oahu provides an incredible opportunity to **connect with the island's past** while appreciating its vibrant present.

Endless Outdoor Adventures for Every Type of Traveler

For those seeking **adventure and exploration**, Oahu is an outdoor paradise with countless activities:

- **Hiking**:
    - *Diamond Head Crater* – A famous hike offering panoramic views of Honolulu and the Pacific Ocean.
    - *Koko Head Stairs* – A challenging 1,048-step climb with rewarding views at the top.
    - *Lanikai Pillbox Hike* – A short but scenic trail leading to breathtaking sunrise views over the Mokulua Islands.
    - *Manoa Falls Trail* – A lush rainforest hike leading to a stunning 150-foot waterfall.
- **Water Activities**:
    - *Snorkeling at Hanauma Bay* – Explore vibrant coral reefs teeming with marine life.
    - *Shark Cage Diving in Haleiwa* – An exhilarating experience with Hawaii's ocean predators (from the safety of a cage).
    - *Kayaking to the Mokulua Islands* – Paddle across crystal-clear waters to explore hidden coves and sea turtle habitats.
    - *Whale Watching* – During winter, spot majestic humpback whales migrating through Hawaiian waters.
- **Extreme Activities**:
    - *Skydiving Over the North Shore* – Free-fall from thousands of feet with unmatched island views.
    - *Ziplining through Lush Valleys* – Soar above forests and waterfalls for an unforgettable thrill.

For adventure seekers, Oahu is a **playground of natural wonders**, offering activities that cater to all skill levels and interests.

A Food Lover's Paradise: Taste the Flavors of Hawaii

Oahu's **culinary scene is a delicious mix of traditional Hawaiian flavors, fresh seafood, and international influences**. From food trucks to fine dining, here's what you can't miss:

- **Poke** – Fresh, cubed raw fish seasoned with soy sauce, sesame oil, and Hawaiian sea salt.
- **Garlic Shrimp** – A North Shore specialty, best enjoyed from a roadside food truck.
- **Loco Moco** – A Hawaiian comfort dish of rice, hamburger patty, fried egg, and rich brown gravy.
- **Malasadas** – Portuguese-inspired, sugar-dusted doughnuts from Leonard's Bakery.
- **Shave Ice** – A refreshing island treat topped with tropical fruit syrups.
- **Huli Huli Chicken** – A flavorful, grilled Hawaiian-style barbecue chicken.
- **Hawaiian Plate Lunch** – A combination of rice, mac salad, and a protein like kalua pork or teriyaki beef.

From **casual beachfront eateries** to **high-end farm-to-table restaurants**, Oahu's food scene will leave your taste buds craving more.

A Year-Round Destination with Amazing Weather

Oahu enjoys **beautiful weather all year**, with warm temperatures and gentle trade winds. The island experiences two main seasons:

- **Summer (May–October)** – Hot and dry, perfect for beach activities and water sports.
- **Winter (November–April)** – Mild and slightly cooler, bringing big waves to the North Shore and ideal conditions for whale watching.

Even during the **rainy season**, showers are usually short-lived, and the sun quickly reappears. No matter when you visit, Oahu offers a **tropical paradise with ideal conditions for outdoor fun**.

A Destination for Every Type of Traveler

Oahu is **one of the most versatile destinations in the world**, catering to all kinds of travelers:

- **Families** – Kid-friendly beaches, interactive museums, and fun attractions like the Honolulu Zoo.

- **Couples** – Romantic sunset cruises, secluded beaches, and fine dining with ocean views.
- **Solo Travelers** – Safe, welcoming environment with plenty of opportunities for adventure.
- **Luxury Seekers** – High-end resorts, world-class spas, and designer shopping.
- **Backpackers** – Budget-friendly hostels, affordable food trucks, and easy-to-navigate public transport.

No matter your **travel style or budget**, Oahu has an experience tailored just for you.

Summary: Why Oahu Belongs on Your Travel List

- A perfect mix of city life and natural beauty
- World-famous beaches and stunning coastlines
- Rich history, Hawaiian culture, and heritage sites
- Endless outdoor adventures for every skill level
- Incredible local cuisine with diverse flavors
- Year-round tropical climate for an ideal getaway
- Something for every traveler—families, couples, adventurers, and food lovers

Oahu is more than just an island—it's an **experience that stays with you long after you leave**. Whether you're drawn by its history, adventure, or simply the warm aloha spirit, Oahu promises memories that will last a lifetime.

1.2 A Brief History of Oahu

Oahu's history is a fascinating tale of ancient Polynesian voyagers, powerful Hawaiian kings, Western explorers, and modern global influences. As the most historically significant island in Hawaii, Oahu has been the center of political power, cultural exchange, and pivotal events that shaped not only the Hawaiian Islands but also the world.

Ancient Polynesian Settlers and Early Hawaiian Society

The first settlers of Oahu arrived around **500–800 AD**, navigating thousands of miles across the Pacific in double-hulled canoes using only the stars and ocean currents for guidance. These **Polynesian voyagers**, believed to have come from the Marquesas Islands and later Tahiti, brought with them the foundational elements of Hawaiian culture—**language, traditions, agriculture, and spirituality**.

By the time Western explorers arrived, Oahu had developed a highly organized **chiefdom society**, ruled by **aliʻi (chiefs)** who governed different districts. The

Hawaiian people thrived under a system known as the **kapu system**, a set of strict laws that governed daily life, religious practices, and social hierarchy.

The island's **fertile valleys, fresh water sources, and abundant fishing grounds** supported a growing population, and the Hawaiians established **extensive taro farms, fishponds, and terraced agriculture**. The largest settlements were in places like Waikīkī, which was once an **important royal retreat** with freshwater streams flowing from the mountains to the sea.

The Unification of Hawaii Under King Kamehameha I

Before the late 1700s, Oahu was ruled by various chiefs who often fought for power. However, everything changed with the arrival of **King Kamehameha I**, who sought to **unify all the Hawaiian Islands under one rule**.

In **1795**, Kamehameha launched a **fierce battle known as the Battle of Nuʻuanu**. His warriors, after intense fighting, **pushed Oahu's defending forces off the cliffs of Nuʻuanu Pali**, securing his control over the island. This victory was a critical step in the **unification of Hawaii**, making Kamehameha the first ruler of the Kingdom of Hawaii.

Following unification, Oahu became a hub of **trade, governance, and cultural transformation** as Hawaii entered a new era of global contact.

The Arrival of Western Explorers and Missionaries

The **first Western contact** with Oahu came in **1778**, when British explorer **Captain James Cook** arrived in Hawaii. Though he never set foot on Oahu, his presence marked the beginning of increased foreign interaction.

By the early 1800s, **traders, whalers, and missionaries** began arriving in large numbers. This period brought:

- **New technologies and goods**, such as metal tools and firearms, which altered traditional Hawaiian warfare.
- **The introduction of Christianity**, as American Protestant missionaries sought to convert the Hawaiian people. This led to **the decline of ancient Hawaiian religious practices** and the construction of Christian churches across Oahu.
- **A shift in land ownership**, with the traditional Hawaiian communal land system changing under the **Great Māhele (1848 land division law)**, which drastically reduced native Hawaiian landholdings.

By the mid-1800s, Oahu had become the **political and economic center of the Hawaiian Kingdom**, with Honolulu emerging as a **thriving port city**.

The Overthrow of the Hawaiian Monarchy

One of the darkest chapters in Oahu's history was the **1893 overthrow of Queen Lili'uokalani**, Hawaii's last reigning monarch.

- A group of **American businessmen and sugar plantation owners**, with the support of the **U.S. government**, staged a coup and took control of the Hawaiian government.
- Queen Lili'uokalani, advocating for her people, **peacefully surrendered to avoid bloodshed**, hoping for later restoration.
- In **1898**, Hawaii was officially **annexed by the United States**, despite strong opposition from Native Hawaiians.

This event led to the eventual **territorial status of Hawaii in 1900** and later **statehood in 1959**.

Pearl Harbor and World War II

Oahu played a **critical role in global history** on **December 7, 1941**, when **Japan launched a surprise attack on Pearl Harbor**, a major U.S. naval base near Honolulu.

- The attack **killed over 2,400 people**, destroyed battleships, and brought the **United States into World War II**.
- Today, the **Pearl Harbor National Memorial** honors those who lost their lives and serves as a reminder of the war's impact on Hawaii and the world.

During the war, Oahu's population surged as thousands of American military personnel were stationed here. This set the stage for Hawaii's post-war economic growth and cultural shifts.

Oahu's Path to Statehood and Modern Development

Following World War II, **Hawaii's push for statehood gained momentum**, and in **1959, Hawaii officially became the 50th U.S. state**. This new status led to:

- A **boom in tourism**, as visitors from the U.S. mainland and beyond flocked to Waikiki's beaches.
- A **military presence that remains strong today**, with Oahu home to several U.S. military bases.

- Rapid **urban development**, making Honolulu a modern city with high-rises, shopping centers, and a growing multicultural community.

Despite modernization, **Oahu continues to honor its Hawaiian roots** through cultural preservation efforts, Hawaiian language revival, and the protection of sacred sites.

The Oahu of Today: Balancing Tradition and Progress

Today, Oahu is a dynamic island that blends **ancient Hawaiian traditions with contemporary life**. It remains the **political, economic, and cultural heart of Hawaii**, attracting visitors who come to experience its:

- **Rich history**, from ancient temples to royal palaces.
- **Stunning landscapes**, from lush valleys to volcanic craters.
- **Diverse cultures**, with influences from Hawaiian, Asian, and Western traditions.

Efforts to **preserve Hawaiian identity** continue, with organizations dedicated to **protecting sacred sites, teaching the Hawaiian language, and reviving traditional practices like hula and wayfinding**.

Summary: Oahu's Historical Journey

- **Settled by Polynesians** over a thousand years ago, Oahu became a thriving Hawaiian society.
- **King Kamehameha I unified the Hawaiian Islands** in 1795 after the famous **Battle of Nuʻuanu**.
- **Western explorers, missionaries, and traders** transformed Oahu's society and economy in the 19th century.
- **The Hawaiian monarchy was overthrown in 1893**, leading to Hawaii's annexation by the U.S. in 1898.
- **The attack on Pearl Harbor in 1941** played a pivotal role in World War II.
- **Hawaii became a U.S. state in 1959**, marking the beginning of a modern tourism-driven economy.
- **Oahu today balances modern development with efforts to preserve Hawaiian culture and traditions.**

Oahu's **rich and complex history** has shaped it into an island where the past meets the present. Visitors can explore this legacy through its **historical sites, cultural festivals, and interactions with the local community**—ensuring that the spirit of old Hawaii continues to thrive.

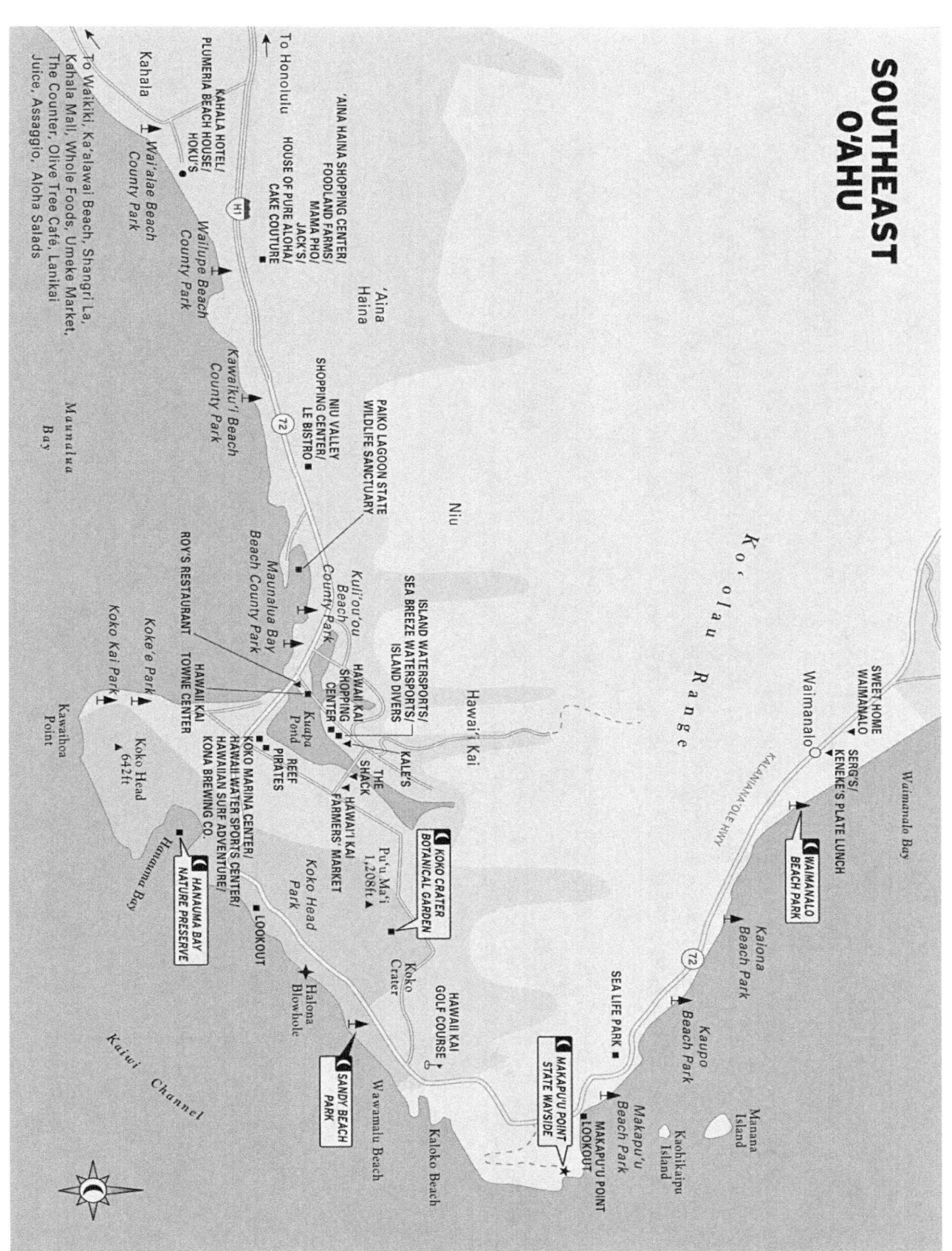

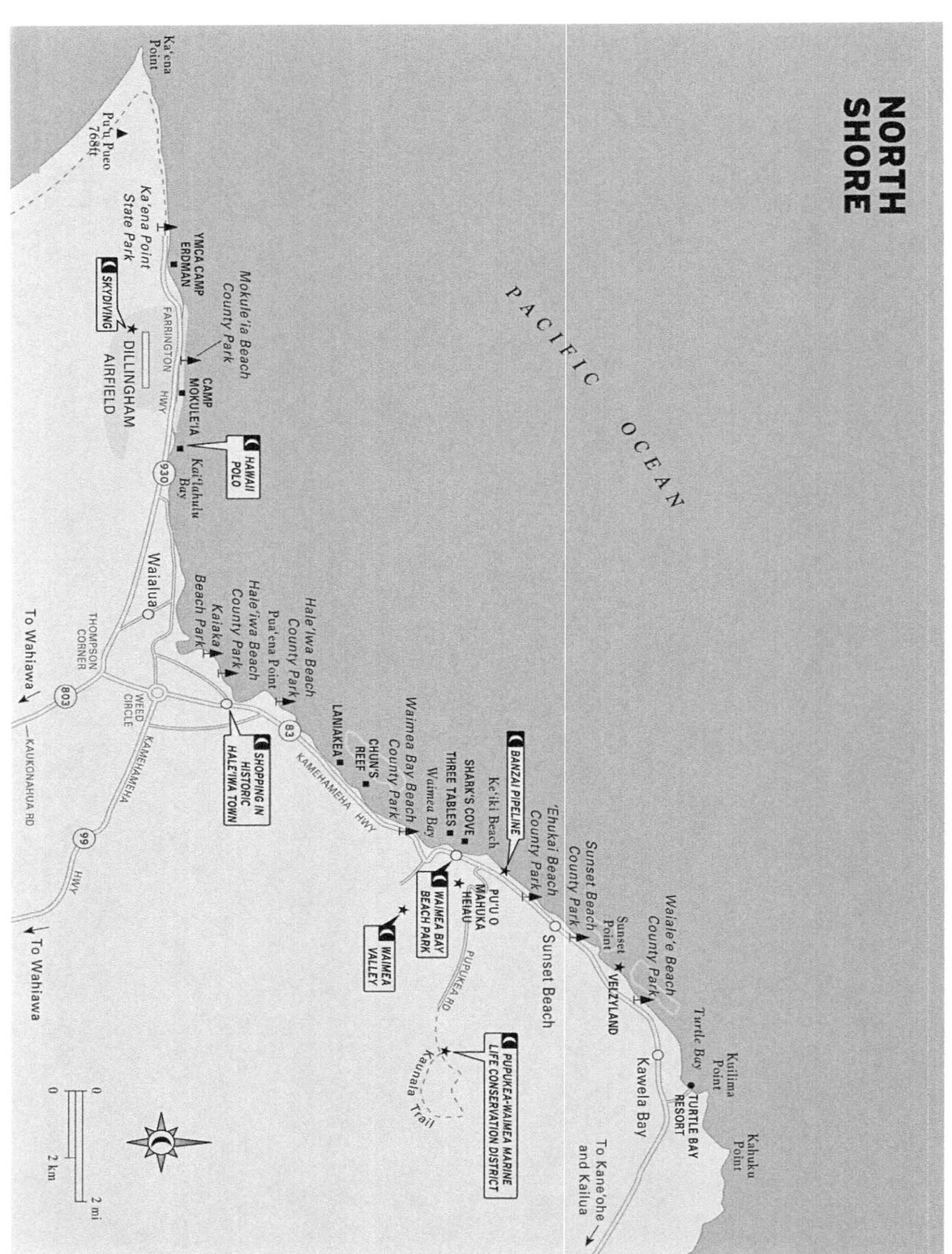

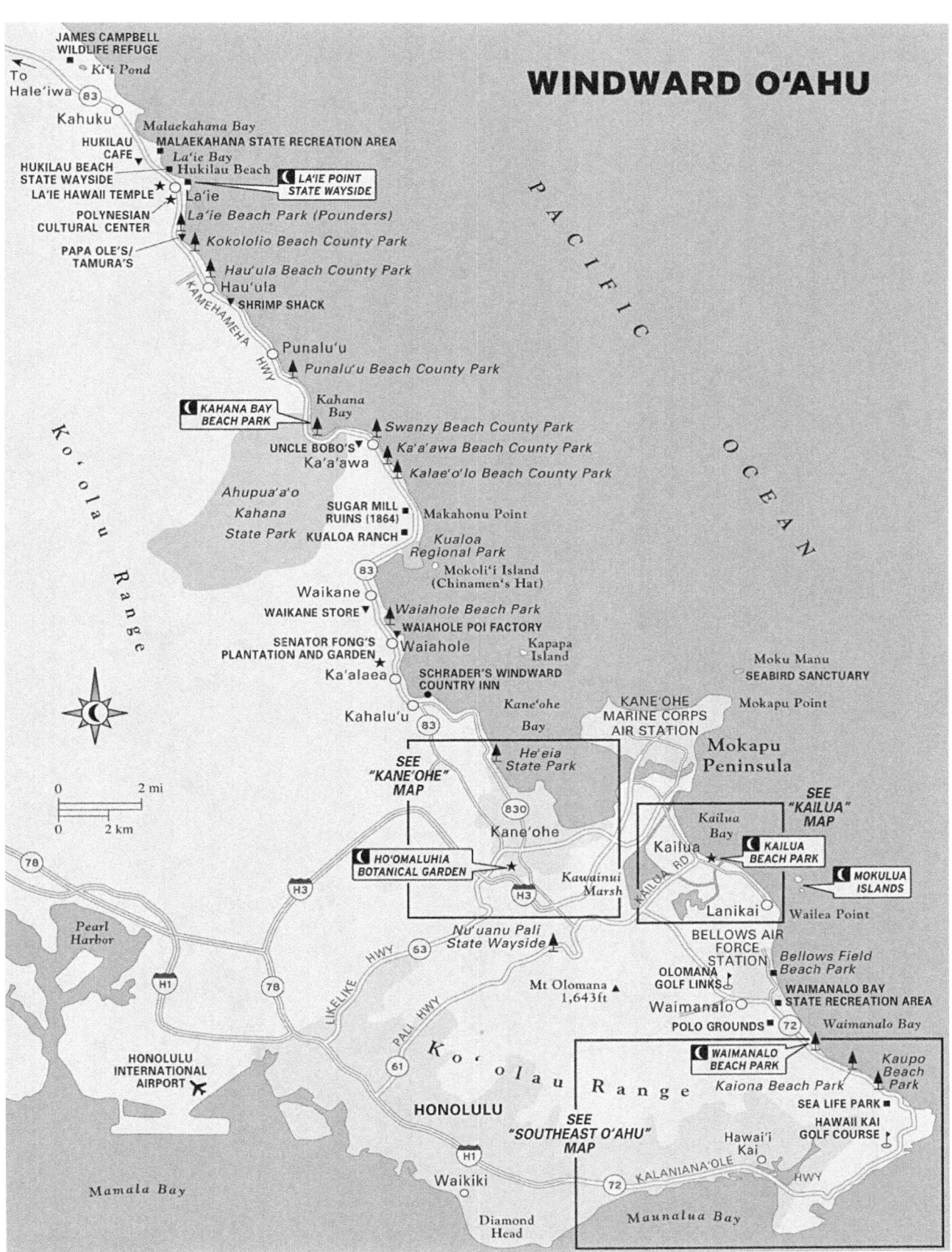

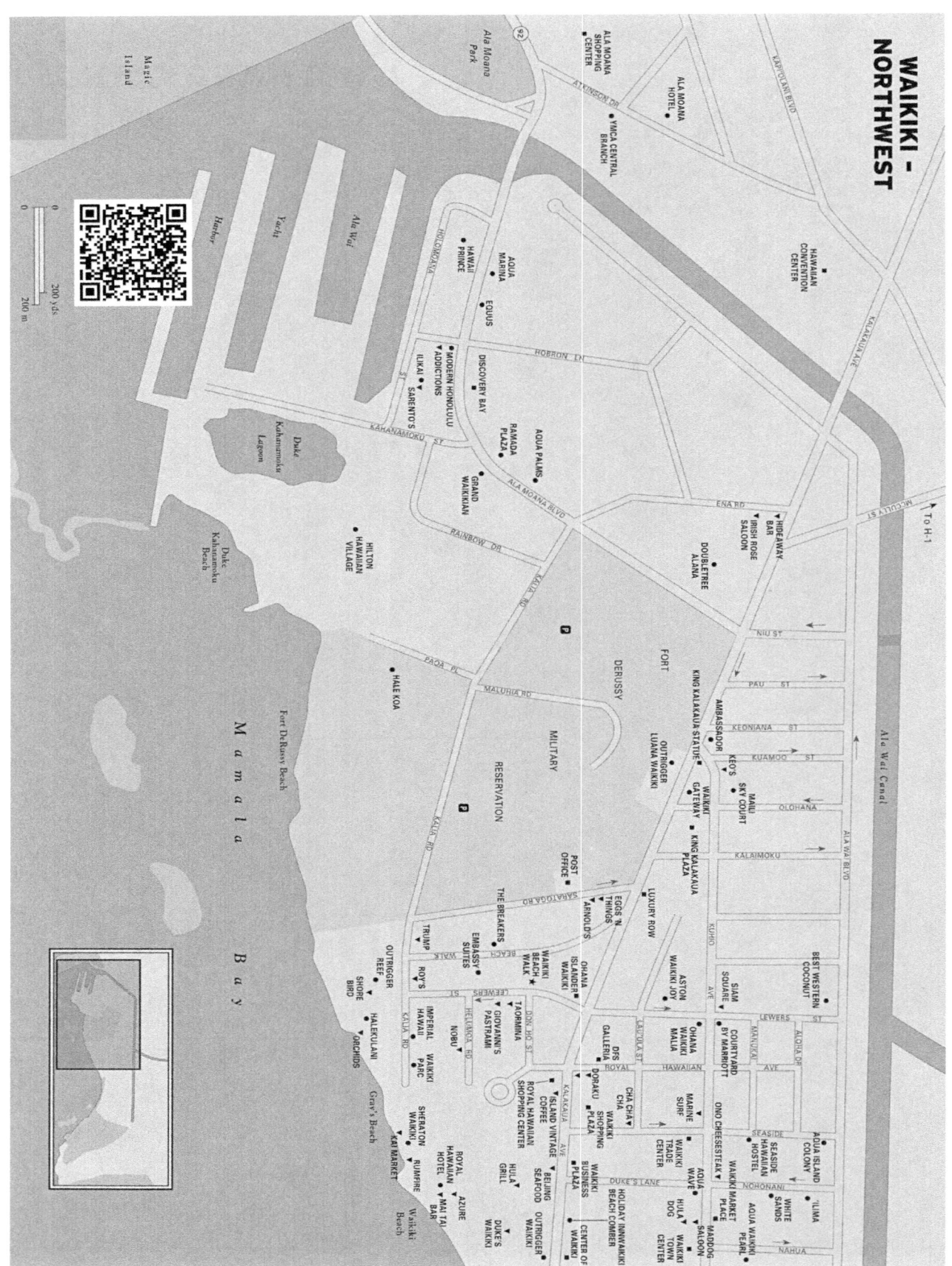

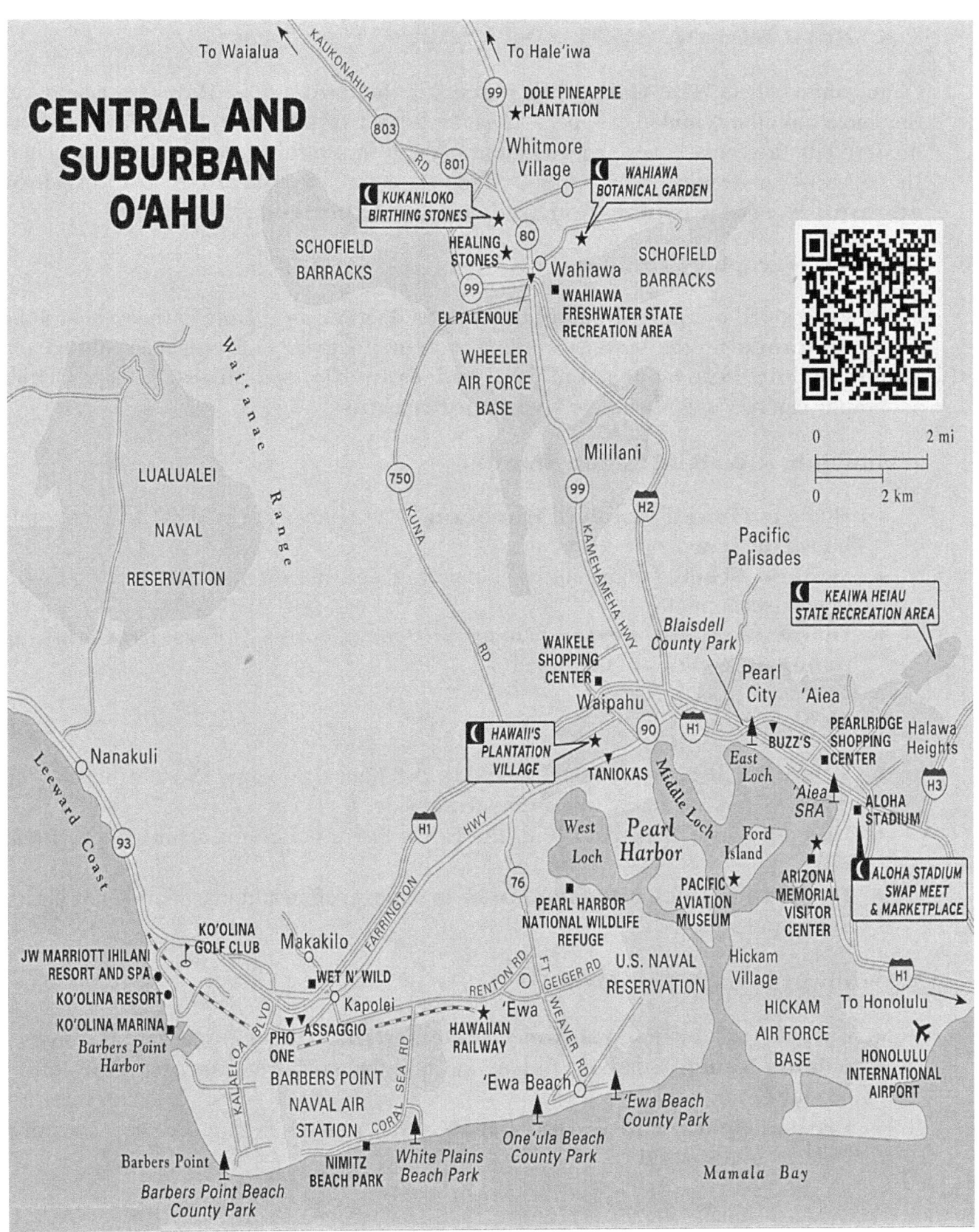

1.3 Oahu's Geography and Climate

Oahu, often called **"The Gathering Place,"** is the third-largest Hawaiian island but the most populous and developed. It is an island of **stunning contrasts**, where modern city life coexists with rugged mountains, lush rainforests, and pristine beaches. Its diverse geography and unique climate create **a paradise for outdoor adventures, scenic exploration, and cultural experiences**.

Oahu's Geographic Features

Oahu was formed by two **shield volcanoes**, the **Wai'anae Range** in the west and the **Ko'olau Range** in the east. Over time, volcanic activity and erosion sculpted the island's **iconic landscapes, valleys, and dramatic coastlines**. Today, Oahu's geography can be categorized into **five major regions**:

1. Honolulu & Waikiki (South Shore)

- Home to **Hawaii's capital, Honolulu**, this region is the political and economic hub of the state.
- **Waikiki Beach**, famous for its golden sand and vibrant nightlife, draws millions of tourists annually.
- **Diamond Head Crater**, an extinct volcanic cone, offers **breathtaking panoramic views** of the island.

2. North Shore

- Known for **legendary surf breaks** like Banzai Pipeline, Sunset Beach, and Waimea Bay, attracting top surfers worldwide.
- Less developed than Honolulu, the North Shore maintains a **laid-back, local vibe**.
- **Lush landscapes and farmlands**, including coffee and macadamia nut farms, define the area.

3. Windward Coast (East Oahu)

- Characterized by **lush rainforests, steep cliffs, and scenic coastal drives**.
- **Kualoa Ranch**, a famous filming location for movies like *Jurassic Park*, offers eco-adventures.
- **Lanikai Beach and Kailua Beach**, often ranked among the most beautiful beaches in the world.

4. Leeward Coast (West Oahu)

- **Drier and sunnier** than other parts of Oahu, with stunning beaches like **Makaha Beach** and **Ko Olina Lagoons**.
- Home to **luxury resorts like the Four Seasons and Disney's Aulani**.
- **Less crowded and more local**, offering an off-the-beaten-path experience.

5. Central Oahu

- Dominated by **plantations, farmlands, and military bases**.
- The historic town of **Wahiawā**, home to **Dole Plantation**, where visitors can learn about Hawaii's pineapple industry.
- Acts as a gateway between the island's urban south and rural north.

Oahu's Climate: What to Expect Year-Round

Oahu enjoys a **tropical climate**, with **warm temperatures, cooling trade winds, and occasional rain showers**. The island is divided into **two primary climate regions**:

- **Windward Side (East & North Oahu)**: Receives **more rain**, making it lush and green.
- **Leeward Side (West & South Oahu)**: Drier and sunnier, with **less rainfall year-round**.

Seasonal Weather Patterns

Season	Temperature (°F)	Rainfall	Notes
Winter (Dec–Feb)	65–80°F	Moderate	Peak surfing season on the North Shore. Higher rainfall in rainforests.
Spring (Mar–May)	68–82°F	Low to moderate	Wildflowers bloom, fewer crowds.
Summer (Jun–Aug)	72–88°F	Low	Warmest months, best for swimming and snorkeling.
Fall (Sep–Nov)	70–86°F	Low to moderate	Pleasant weather, fewer tourists.

Trade Winds and Kona Winds

- **Trade Winds (Most of the Year)**: Blow from the **northeast**, bringing **cooling breezes and mild temperatures**.
- **Kona Winds (Occasionally in Winter and Fall)**: Blow from the **southwest**, causing **hotter, humid weather and vog (volcanic haze)** from the Big Island.

Best Time to Visit Oahu Based on Climate

- **For Beach Lovers & Sun Seekers** → **April to October** (Dry season, warmest weather).
- **For Surfers** → **November to February** (Peak surf season on the North Shore).
- **For Hikers & Outdoor Activities** → **March to May, September to November** (Mild weather, fewer crowds).
- **For Budget Travelers** → **Spring & Fall shoulder seasons** (Lower prices, good weather).

Summary: Understanding Oahu's Geography and Climate

- Oahu's landscape includes **two mountain ranges, scenic coastlines, and famous beaches**.
- The island has **five distinct regions**, each offering **unique experiences and natural beauty**.
- The climate is **tropical and warm year-round**, with **trade winds keeping temperatures comfortable**.
- The **Windward side is wetter and greener**, while the **Leeward side is drier and sunnier**.
- The **best time to visit depends on your interests**, whether it's surfing, hiking, or relaxing on the beach.

With its **stunning geography and ideal climate**, Oahu offers **year-round opportunities for adventure, relaxation, and cultural exploration**. Whether you're hiking up **Diamond Head, surfing at Sunset Beach, or relaxing on the white sands of Lanikai,** you'll experience the best of Hawaii's natural beauty.

1.4 Best Time to Visit Oahu

Oahu is a **year-round destination** with warm temperatures, beautiful beaches, and diverse activities no matter when you visit. However, the **best time to visit** depends on your interests—whether you're looking for **ideal beach weather, thrilling surf, fewer crowds, or budget-friendly travel.**

Understanding Oahu's Seasons

Unlike mainland destinations, Oahu does not have **dramatic seasonal changes**. Instead, it experiences two primary seasons:

1. Dry Season (April – October)

- **Weather:** Warm, sunny, and dry with minimal rainfall.
- **Ocean Conditions:** Calmer waters, especially on the North Shore.
- **Best For:** Swimming, snorkeling, hiking, and outdoor activities.
- **Events:** Honolulu Festival (March), Lantern Floating Festival (May), and the Pan-Pacific Festival (June).

2. Wet Season (November – March)

- **Weather:** Mild temperatures, occasional rain, and lush green landscapes.
- **Ocean Conditions: North Shore waves are massive**, attracting pro surfers, while **South Shore remains calm**.
- **Best For:** Surfing, whale watching, and cultural festivals.
- **Events:** Vans Triple Crown of Surfing (Nov-Dec), Honolulu Marathon (Dec), and Chinese New Year celebrations (Jan-Feb).

Best Time to Visit Based on Interests

1. For the Best Beach Weather: May – September

- **Why?** The warmest, sunniest months with minimal rainfall.
- **Where? Waikiki Beach, Lanikai Beach, and Ko Olina Lagoons** offer perfect conditions for swimming and sunbathing.
- **What to Expect?** Ideal for water sports like **snorkeling, paddleboarding, and diving.**

2. For Surfing: November – February

- **Why?** North Shore waves reach **20-30 feet**, attracting the world's best surfers.

- **Where?** **Banzai Pipeline, Waimea Bay, and Sunset Beach** host major competitions.
- **What to Expect?** Thrilling surf contests, but **not ideal for casual swimming** due to strong currents.

3. For Whale Watching: December – April

- **Why?** Humpback whales migrate from Alaska to Hawaii's warm waters.
- **Where? Makapu'u Point, Waianae Coast, and Diamond Head Lookout** are great viewing spots.
- **What to Expect?** Scenic boat tours and **incredible whale breaches** along the coast.

4. For Hiking and Outdoor Activities: March – June & September – November

- **Why?** Pleasant temperatures, **fewer crowds**, and lush green landscapes after the rainy season.
- **Where? Diamond Head, Koko Crater Trail, and Manoa Falls** offer stunning views.
- **What to Expect?** Cooler weather for hikes, **vibrant flora**, and **less crowded trails**.

5. For Avoiding Crowds: Mid-April – Early June & September – Mid-November

- **Why?** These are the **off-peak seasons**, meaning **cheaper hotels, fewer tourists, and better availability for tours**.
- **Where?** Popular spots like **Hanauma Bay, Pearl Harbor, and Waikiki Beach** are much less crowded.
- **What to Expect?** A more **relaxed, authentic island experience**.

6. For Budget Travelers: Late April – Early June & Late September – Early December

- **Why? Lower airfare and hotel rates** as demand drops between peak travel periods.
- **Where? Waikiki hotels and North Shore vacation rentals** offer great deals.
- **What to Expect? Fewer tourists, discounts on activities, and affordable flight options**.

Month-by-Month Guide

Month	Weather	Crowds	Events & Activities
January	Warm, some rain	Moderate	**Whale watching**, Chinese New Year
February	Warm, occasional rain	Low to moderate	**Surfing, whale watching**
March	Warm, light rain	Moderate	Honolulu Festival
April	Warmer, less rain	Low to moderate	Peak **snorkeling and hiking** season
May	Hot, dry	Low	Lantern Floating Festival
June	Hot, sunny	Moderate	Pan-Pacific Festival
July	Hot, humid	High	4th of July fireworks, Bon Dance festivals
August	Very hot	High	Obon Festival, Duke's OceanFest
September	Warm, less humid	Low	Aloha Festivals

October	Warm, dry	Low	Hawaii Food & Wine Festival
November	Mild, wetter	Moderate	Vans Triple Crown Surfing
December	Warm, occasional rain	High	Honolulu Marathon, Christmas events

Summary: When Should You Visit Oahu?

- For sun & beaches → May – September
- For surfing → November – February
- For whale watching → December – April
- For hiking & exploring → March – June & September – November
- For avoiding crowds & saving money → April – Early June & September – November

Oahu is **stunning year-round**, but the best time depends on **your travel goals**. Whether you're catching waves, hiking scenic trails, or relaxing on pristine beaches, **there's no bad time to visit this tropical paradise.**

Chapter 2. Getting to and Around Oahu

2.1 Flights to Oahu: International and Domestic Airports

Oahu is the main gateway to Hawaii, with **Daniel K. Inouye International Airport (HNL)** in Honolulu serving as the island's primary airport. Whether you're flying from **the U.S. mainland, Asia, or other international destinations,** Oahu is **well-connected** with frequent flights and reliable airline options.

Daniel K. Inouye International Airport (HNL)

- **Location:** Honolulu, about **6 miles (10 km) from Waikiki**
- **Airport Code:** HNL
- **Terminals:**
    - **Terminal 1:** Hawaiian Airlines (interisland and mainland U.S. flights)
    - **Terminal 2:** Most **international and domestic flights**
    - **Terminal 3:** Smaller interisland carriers

Airlines Serving HNL

From the U.S. Mainland

- **Hawaiian Airlines:** Direct flights from major cities like **Los Angeles, San Francisco, Seattle, and New York**
- **Alaska Airlines:** Serves **Seattle, Portland, and California** cities
- **American Airlines:** Flights from **Dallas, Los Angeles, and Phoenix**
- **Delta Airlines:** Routes from **Atlanta, Los Angeles, Seattle, and Salt Lake City**
- **Southwest Airlines:** Budget-friendly flights from **California and Las Vegas**
- **United Airlines:** Direct routes from **Denver, Chicago, San Francisco, and Houston**

International Flights

- **Japan Airlines & ANA:** Direct flights from **Tokyo, Osaka, and Nagoya**
- **Korean Air & Asiana Airlines:** Routes from **Seoul**
- **Air Canada & WestJet:** Flights from **Vancouver and Toronto**
- **Qantas & Jetstar:** Direct flights from **Sydney, Melbourne, and Brisbane**
- **Philippine Airlines:** Manila to Honolulu route

Interisland Flights

If you're visiting multiple Hawaiian islands, **short interisland flights** are available:

- **Hawaiian Airlines:** Most frequent interisland flights
- **Southwest Airlines:** Budget-friendly option for interisland travel
- **Mokulele Airlines:** Small aircraft flights to Maui, Big Island, and Molokai

Flight times between islands are **typically 30–50 minutes**.

Arriving at HNL: What to Expect

Customs & Immigration (For International Travelers)

- U.S. citizens arriving from the mainland **do not need to go through customs**.
- International visitors **must pass through U.S. immigration** upon arrival.

Transportation from HNL to Waikiki and Other Areas

Once you land at **HNL**, you have several options to reach **Waikiki, Ko Olina, or the North Shore**:

1. **Taxi & Ride-Sharing (Uber/Lyft)**
   - **Cost:** ~$30-$45 to Waikiki
   - **Time:** ~20–30 minutes
   - **Best for:** Convenience and direct service
2. **Airport Shuttles**
   - **Cost:** ~$15-$20 per person
   - **Time:** 30–40 minutes (shared rides)
   - **Best for:** Budget travelers
3. **Public Bus (TheBus)**
   - **Routes:** #19, #20, and #31 serve Waikiki
   - **Cost:** $3 per ride
   - **Time:** ~1 hour
   - **Best for:** Budget-conscious travelers with light luggage
4. **Rental Cars**
   - Available from **Avis, Budget, Enterprise, Hertz, and Alamo**
   - **Best for:** Travelers planning to explore beyond Waikiki

Summary

- **Daniel K. Inouye International Airport (HNL)** is Oahu's main airport, with frequent **domestic and international flights**.
- **Flights from the U.S. mainland** are available from **Los Angeles, San Francisco, Seattle, New York, and more**.
- **International connections** include flights from **Japan, South Korea, Australia, and Canada**.
- **Interisland flights** allow quick access to Maui, Kauai, and the Big Island.
- **Ground transportation options** include **taxis, shuttles, public buses, and rental cars** for easy access to Waikiki and beyond.

2.2 Transportation Options: Renting a Car, Public Transit, and Ride-Sharing

Getting around Oahu is **relatively easy**, with multiple transportation options to suit different travel styles and budgets. Whether you **prefer the freedom of a rental car, the affordability of public transit, or the convenience of ride-sharing**, Oahu offers a variety of ways to explore its stunning landscapes, vibrant neighborhoods, and top attractions.

Renting a Car: Is It Worth It?

Pros:

■ **Freedom & Flexibility:** Drive at your own pace and visit off-the-beaten-path destinations.
■ **Convenience for Exploring Beyond Waikiki:** Best for travelers planning to visit **North Shore, Ko Olina, and the Windward Coast**.
■ **Scenic Drives:** Ideal for experiencing routes like **Tantalus Drive, Pali Highway, and Kamehameha Highway**.

Cons:

✘ **Traffic Congestion:** Honolulu and Waikiki experience heavy traffic, especially during rush hours.
✘ **Expensive Parking:** Hotels charge around **$30-$50 per night** for parking.
✘ **Not Needed for Waikiki:** If staying in **Waikiki**, many attractions are within walking distance or accessible via **TheBus**.

Where to Rent a Car

- **Daniel K. Inouye International Airport (HNL):** Most major rental companies are available, including **Alamo, Hertz, Enterprise, Avis, Budget, and National**.
- **Waikiki Locations:** Several agencies have branches in **Waikiki**, allowing you to rent for just a few days instead of your entire stay.

Driving Tips for Oahu

- **Speed limits** are lower than on the mainland, typically **35-45 mph (56-72 km/h) on highways**.
- **Parking is limited** in Honolulu and popular beaches like Lanikai and Waikiki. Consider using **paid garages** or arriving early.

- **Traffic congestion** is common on **H-1 Freeway and in Waikiki** from 7 AM–9 AM and 3 PM–6 PM.

Best For: Travelers planning to explore **North Shore, Ko Olina, and secluded beaches**.

Public Transit: TheBus

Oahu's public bus system, **TheBus**, is an affordable and reliable way to get around, covering most of the island, including **Honolulu, Waikiki, North Shore, and Windward Coast**.

Key Information

- **Fare:** $3 per ride / $7.50 for a 1-day pass / $80 for a monthly pass
- **Payment:** Cash (exact fare) or the **HOLO Card** (reloadable transit card)
- **Frequency:** Every 15-30 minutes in urban areas, but **less frequent in rural regions**

Popular Routes for Tourists

- **Route 20:** Airport → Pearl Harbor → Ala Moana → Waikiki
- **Route 60:** Honolulu → North Shore → Haleiwa → Turtle Bay
- **Route 52:** Honolulu → Wahiawa → North Shore (scenic route)
- **Route 23:** Waikiki → Hanauma Bay → Sea Life Park

Pros:
- **Cheap and reliable**
- **Covers most of Oahu**
- **Eco-friendly option**

Cons:
- ✘ **Slow travel times** compared to cars
- ✘ **Limited service to remote areas**
- ✘ **Can be crowded, especially during peak hours**

Best For: Budget-conscious travelers staying mainly in **Waikiki and Honolulu**.

Ride-Sharing: Uber & Lyft

Uber and Lyft operate throughout Oahu and are great alternatives to renting a car, especially for **short distances or getting around Waikiki and Honolulu**.

Estimated Fares

- **HNL Airport to Waikiki:** ~$30-$45
- **Waikiki to Pearl Harbor:** ~$40-$50
- **Waikiki to North Shore:** ~$100-$120
- **Waikiki to Hanauma Bay:** ~$35-$45

Tips for Using Ride-Sharing

- **Surge pricing** applies during peak hours, especially in **Waikiki and the airport**.
- Consider using **UberPOOL/Lyft Shared** to save on costs.
- Drivers are **plentiful in Waikiki and Honolulu** but may take longer to arrive in remote areas.

Best For: Travelers who **don't want to rent a car** but need occasional private transportation.

Other Transportation Options

Taxis

- Available at hotels, airports, and major tourist sites.
- **More expensive than Uber/Lyft** (Waikiki to Airport: ~$45-$55).
- Best for **travelers without a smartphone or those needing an immediate ride**.

Biki (Bike Sharing)

- **Biki Stations** throughout Honolulu and Waikiki.
- **Rates:** $4.50 per ride or $12 for a 3-hour pass.
- Best for **short-distance travel within Honolulu and Waikiki**.

Mopeds & Scooters

- **Rental Companies:** Hawaiian Style Rentals, Scoot Coupe
- **Cost:** ~$40 per day
- Best for **short, scenic rides around Waikiki and Diamond Head**.

Summary

- **Renting a car** is **ideal for exploring beyond Honolulu**, but parking and traffic can be challenges.

- **TheBus** is **affordable and covers most of Oahu**, but it's slower than driving.
- **Ride-sharing (Uber/Lyft)** is **convenient for short trips** but costly for long distances.
- **Biki bike rentals and mopeds** offer **fun alternatives** for short-distance travel.

For most travelers, a **mix of public transit, ride-sharing, and occasional rentals** is the best way to explore Oahu efficiently.

2.3 Navigating the Island: Road Rules and Travel Tips

Driving in Oahu can be an enjoyable experience, especially with its **scenic coastal highways, lush mountain roads, and historic towns**. However, the island has unique road rules, local customs, and potential traffic challenges that visitors should be aware of. This guide provides **essential road rules, practical tips, and local insights** to help you navigate Oahu smoothly and safely.

Road Rules in Oahu

1. Speed Limits & Traffic Laws

- **Highways:** 45–55 mph (72–88 km/h)
- **Urban Areas:** 25–35 mph (40–56 km/h)
- **Residential Zones & School Areas:** 20–25 mph (32–40 km/h)
- **Strict Seat Belt Laws:** Everyone in the vehicle must wear a seatbelt.
- **No Handheld Devices:** Using a cellphone while driving is illegal unless hands-free.

2. Traffic Flow & Driving Style

- **Traffic moves slower than on the mainland**—locals often drive at or below the speed limit.
- **Left lane = faster-moving traffic**, but not everyone follows this strictly.
- **Yield to pedestrians**—crosswalks are strictly enforced.
- **Be patient with merging traffic**—locals are generally courteous, and you should be too.

3. Stop Signs & Intersections

- **No right turn on red** in many places (check for signage).
- **Four-way stop intersections:** The first vehicle to arrive goes first.

4. Parking Rules & Fees

- **Street Parking:** Marked by signs; illegal parking results in towing.
- **Hotel Parking:** Costs **$30-$50 per night** in Waikiki.
- **Beach Parking:** Arrive early to secure spots at **Lanikai, Kailua, and Sunset Beach**.

Key Roads & Scenic Drives in Oahu

1. H-1, H-2, and H-3 Freeways

- **H-1:** Runs through Honolulu and Waikiki—often congested during rush hours.
- **H-2:** Leads north to **Wahiawa and North Shore**.
- **H-3:** One of the most scenic highways, connecting **Honolulu to Kaneohe**.

2. Kamehameha Highway (Route 83)

- **The most famous scenic drive on Oahu**—runs along the North Shore.
- Passes by **Dole Plantation, Waimea Bay, and Turtle Beach**.

3. Pali Highway (Route 61)

- Connects **Honolulu to the Windward side** with stunning views.
- Stop at the **Nuʻuanu Pali Lookout** for panoramic views.

4. Farrington Highway (Route 93)

- Leads to **Kaʻena Point**, the remote westernmost tip of Oahu.
- A great route for sunset views, but **no gas stations or stores nearby**.

Traffic & Peak Travel Times

Oahu, particularly **Honolulu and Waikiki**, experiences **heavy traffic** during peak hours.

Rush Hour Traffic

- **Morning:** 6:30 AM – 9:00 AM (Honolulu-bound)
- **Evening:** 3:30 PM – 6:00 PM (Waikiki and suburbs)
- **Weekends:** Expect congestion near **beaches, Pearl Harbor, and popular tourist sites**.

Tips to Avoid Traffic

✔ **Travel early in the morning** for scenic drives and sightseeing.
✔ **Use alternative routes** (e.g., Pali Highway instead of H-1).
✔ **Stay in Waikiki** if your itinerary focuses on urban attractions.

Local Travel Tips for a Smooth Journey

1. Download Essential Apps

- **Google Maps / Waze:** Real-time traffic updates.
- **Hawaiian 511:** Local road conditions and alerts.
- **TheBus App:** Bus routes and schedules.

2. Respect Local Driving Culture

- **Be courteous:** Locals often let others merge—return the favor.
- **Avoid excessive honking:** It's seen as rude unless for emergencies.
- **Let locals pass on narrow roads**, especially in rural areas.

3. Be Cautious on Rural Roads

- **Single-lane roads** on the North Shore and Windward Coast.
- **Flash flooding risk:** Avoid driving in heavy rain, especially near **Waimea Valley**.

4. Watch for Wildlife & Pedestrians

- **Chickens, wild pigs, and seabirds** sometimes cross roads unexpectedly.
- **Pedestrian crossings are strictly enforced**—always yield to people on crosswalks.

Summary

- **Follow speed limits** (even if locals drive slower).
- **Use H-3, Pali Highway, and Kamehameha Highway** for scenic drives.
- **Avoid traffic by traveling early** and using real-time navigation apps.
- **Respect the island's relaxed driving style**—patience is key.

Chapter 3. Top Attractions in Oahu

3.1 Pearl Harbor and USS Arizona Memorial

Short History

Pearl Harbor is one of the most historically significant sites in the United States. Located on the southern coast of Oahu, this deep-water naval base became a pivotal location in World War II. On the morning of **December 7, 1941**, the Japanese Imperial Navy launched a surprise military attack on Pearl Harbor, leading to the destruction of multiple U.S. Navy battleships, aircraft, and the tragic loss of over **2,400 American lives**. This event prompted the United States' entry into **World War II**.

Among the battleships lost that day was the **USS Arizona**, which exploded and sank within minutes after being hit by armor-piercing bombs. The ship's wreckage remains beneath the waters of Pearl Harbor and serves as a final resting place for over **1,100 sailors** who perished aboard.

Today, Pearl Harbor stands as a place of reflection and remembrance, attracting millions of visitors annually who come to learn about the attack, pay respects to those who lost their lives, and explore the historic sites that commemorate this pivotal moment in world history.

Description

The **USS Arizona Memorial** is the most famous landmark at Pearl Harbor. This **white floating structure**, designed to sit over the sunken battleship without touching it, offers a **solemn and moving experience** for visitors. As you stand on the memorial, you can look down into the waters and see parts of the **USS Arizona** still visible beneath the surface. Oil droplets, often called **"the tears of the Arizona,"** continue to seep from the wreckage, serving as a haunting reminder of the past.

The Pearl Harbor National Memorial is part of a larger historic complex that includes several other significant sites:

- **USS Missouri (Mighty Mo):** This battleship, famously known as the site where **Japan officially surrendered** on **September 2, 1945**, marking the end of World War II, is now a floating museum. Visitors can walk the decks, explore its massive guns, and learn about its role in U.S. naval history.
- **USS Bowfin Submarine Museum & Park:** Dubbed the "Pearl Harbor Avenger," this **World War II-era submarine** served in the Pacific and offers a fascinating look into life aboard a wartime submarine.
- **Pearl Harbor Aviation Museum:** Housed in two historic hangars that survived the 1941 attack, this museum features **dozens of aircraft**, including Japanese planes and American bombers, as well as interactive exhibits detailing aviation's role in WWII.

For visitors, the experience begins at the **Pearl Harbor Visitor Center**, where exhibits, films, and artifacts provide context to the attack and its aftermath. Guests then take a **boat ride to the USS Arizona Memorial**, where they can witness firsthand the final resting place of the fallen sailors.

Visitor Information

📍 **Location**

Pearl Harbor National Memorial
1 Arizona Memorial Place, Honolulu, HI 96818, USA

💰 Price

- **USS Arizona Memorial:** Free (reservation required)
- **USS Missouri Battleship:** $35 for adults, $18 for children
- **USS Bowfin Submarine:** $22 for adults, $12 for children
- **Pearl Harbor Aviation Museum:** $25 for adults, $12 for children
- **Full Pearl Harbor Experience Pass:** ~$90 (includes access to all sites)

🕐 Opening Hours

- **Daily:** 7:00 AM – 5:00 PM
- **Closed on:** Thanksgiving, Christmas, and New Year's Day

🌐 Website

www.nps.gov/perl

🔑 Key Features

◼ **USS Arizona Memorial:** Floating structure built over the sunken battleship
◼ **Battleship Missouri:** Walk the deck where WWII officially ended
◼ **USS Bowfin Submarine:** Explore the interior of a real WWII submarine
◼ **Pearl Harbor Aviation Museum:** See vintage aircraft and wartime artifacts
◼ **Historical Exhibits & Film Presentations:** Gain insight into the attack and its impact
◼ **Boat Tours:** Ride across the harbor to reach the USS Arizona Memorial

🛎 Visitor Services

✔ **Guided Tours & Audio Guides** (available in multiple languages)
✔ **On-Site Museum & Gift Shops**
✔ **Shuttle Service Between Memorials**
✔ **Accessibility Features for Disabled Visitors**
✔ **Cafeteria & Dining Options Nearby**

Summary

A visit to **Pearl Harbor and the USS Arizona Memorial** is an **emotional, educational, and powerful experience**. This historic site not only tells the story of one of the most tragic days in U.S. history but also honors the resilience and sacrifice of those who served. From the hauntingly beautiful **USS Arizona Memorial** to the legendary **Battleship Missouri**, the **submarine Bowfin**, and the **Aviation Museum**, this site offers a **comprehensive look into World War II history**.

For anyone visiting Oahu, Pearl Harbor is a **must-see destination**, providing a deeper understanding of the past and an opportunity to **reflect on the sacrifices made for freedom**.

3.2 Diamond Head State Monument

Short History

Diamond Head, known in Hawaiian as **Lēʻahi**, is one of Oahu's most iconic landmarks. This **extinct volcanic crater** was formed **over 300,000 years ago** during a single explosive eruption. Early Hawaiians named it "Lēʻahi" because the shape of the ridgeline resembled the **dorsal fin of a tuna fish** (*ahi* in Hawaiian).

In the late 19th century, British sailors mistook the **crater's calcite crystals** for diamonds, giving rise to the modern name **Diamond Head**—despite the fact that no diamonds were ever found.

During the **early 1900s**, the U.S. military recognized Diamond Head's strategic location for **coastal defense**. **Fort Ruger**, Hawaii's first military reservation, was built within the crater, complete with bunkers, tunnels, and observation decks. While no battles ever took place here, the **remnants of old military installations** can still be seen along the popular hiking trail today.

Today, Diamond Head is a **Hawaiian State Monument** and one of the most visited attractions on the island, offering breathtaking **panoramic views of Honolulu, Waikiki Beach, and the Pacific Ocean.**

Description

Diamond Head is **best known for its scenic hiking trail**, which leads visitors to the **summit of the crater**. This moderately challenging hike spans **0.8 miles (1.3 km) one way**, with **560 feet (171 m) of elevation gain**. The hike takes approximately **45 minutes to an hour** to reach the top, with rest stops and lookout points along the way.

The **trail begins inside the crater** and winds through **rocky switchbacks, tunnels, and staircases**, including a **99-step staircase** near the summit. Along the way, visitors will pass **old military bunkers and a historic Fire Control Station**, which was used to coordinate artillery defenses in the early 1900s.

At the **summit**, visitors are rewarded with a **spectacular 360-degree view** of Waikiki, downtown Honolulu, and the vast Pacific Ocean. The **sunrise view** from Diamond Head is particularly famous, making early morning hikes extremely popular.

Visitor Information

📍 Location

Diamond Head State Monument
4200 Diamond Head Road, Honolulu, HI 96815, USA

💰 Price

- **Entry Fee:** $5 per person (Hawaii residents enter free)
- **Parking Fee:** $10 per vehicle

⬤ Opening Hours

- **Daily:** 6:00 AM – 6:00 PM
- **Last Hike Entry:** 4:00 PM
- **Closed on:** Christmas and New Year's Day

🌐 Website

www.dlnr.hawaii.gov

🔑 Key Features

- **Scenic Hiking Trail:** 0.8-mile (1.3 km) hike to the summit
- **Panoramic Views:** Overlooks Waikiki Beach, Honolulu, and the Pacific
- **Historical Military Bunkers:** Explore remnants of WWII-era fortifications
- **Sunrise & Sunset Views:** Popular for breathtaking early morning and evening scenery
- **Wildlife & Flora:** Unique crater ecosystem with native Hawaiian plants

🛎 Visitor Services

- ✔ **Restrooms & Water Stations** (near the trailhead)
- ✔ **Food Trucks & Snack Vendors** (outside the entrance)
- ✔ **Interpretive Signs & Educational Exhibits**
- ✔ **Guided Tours Available**
- ✔ **Shaded Rest Areas**

Hiking Tips & Safety Guidelines

- **Start Early:** The trail can get crowded, and the Hawaiian sun can be intense by mid-morning.
- **Wear Comfortable Shoes:** The trail includes uneven terrain, stairs, and a tunnel.
- **Bring Water:** There are no water stations along the trail, only at the entrance.
- **Use Sunscreen & a Hat:** There's little shade along the route.
- **Prepare for a Short Workout:** The incline and staircases can be challenging for some visitors.

Summary

Diamond Head State Monument is an **unmissable attraction** for visitors to Oahu. This historic volcanic crater offers an **adventurous hike, stunning panoramic views**, and a glimpse into **Hawaii's military history**. Whether you're seeking **a rewarding sunrise trek, a scenic workout, or a history-filled adventure**, Diamond Head delivers an experience that **blends nature, history, and incredible vistas**.

3.3 Waikiki Beach and Promenade

Short History

Waikiki Beach is **one of the most famous beaches in the world**, known for its golden sand, gentle waves, and vibrant cityscape. Historically, Waikiki (meaning "spouting water" in Hawaiian) was once a **playground for Hawaiian royalty**. In the 1800s, it was home to lush wetlands and taro fields, with Hawaiian aliʻi (chiefs) using the calm waters for **canoe paddling and early forms of surfing**.

In the early 1900s, **Waikiki transformed into a global vacation hotspot**, thanks to the construction of luxury resorts like the **Moana Surfrider Hotel (1901)** and the **Royal Hawaiian Hotel (1927)**. The beach became synonymous with the legendary **Duke Kahanamoku**, a Hawaiian waterman and Olympic gold medalist who popularized modern surfing. Today, Waikiki remains **the heart of tourism in**

Hawaii, offering a blend of **relaxation, entertainment, and cultural experiences**.

Description

Waikiki Beach stretches **about two miles (3.2 km)** along Honolulu's coast, featuring several distinct sections, each with unique characteristics:

- **Kuhio Beach Park:** Best for beginner surfers, with a protective breakwall creating calm waters.
- **Queen's Surf Beach:** A quieter spot near Kapiolani Park, great for snorkeling and swimming.
- **Fort DeRussy Beach:** A less crowded area near Hilton Hawaiian Village, with a peaceful ambiance.
- **Duke Kahanamoku Beach:** The widest stretch of Waikiki Beach, popular for canoe rides and stand-up paddleboarding.
- **Waikiki Promenade:** A scenic boardwalk lined with palm trees, street performers, shopping outlets, and oceanfront restaurants.

Waikiki is also known for its vibrant nightlife, bustling shopping districts, and numerous cultural events. The **Duke Kahanamoku Statue**, located along the promenade, is a popular landmark where visitors often take photos.

Visitor Information

📍 Location

Waikiki Beach, Honolulu, HI 96815, USA

💰 Price

- **Free to access** (Some areas may charge for rentals or private beach services)

🕐 Opening Hours

- **Open 24/7** (Lifeguards on duty from 9:00 AM – 5:30 PM)

🌐 Website

www.gohawaii.com/waikiki

🔑 Key Features

- ■ **Iconic Surfing Spot:** Gentle waves perfect for beginners
- ■ **Stunning Sunset Views:** A must-see in the evening
- ■ **Duke Kahanamoku Statue:** Tribute to Hawaii's legendary surfer
- ■ **Lively Atmosphere:** Shopping, nightlife, and street entertainment
- ■ **Variety of Beach Activities:** Swimming, stand-up paddleboarding, canoe rides

- ✔ Beachfront Hotels & Resorts
- ✔ Rental Shops for Surfboards & Paddleboards
- ✔ Public Restrooms & Showers
- ✔ Lifeguard Stations
- ✔ Nearby Dining & Shopping

Things to Do at Waikiki Beach

🏄 Try Surfing or Paddleboarding

Waikiki is famous for its **gentle, rolling waves**, making it an ideal spot for first-time surfers. Several surf schools along the beach offer **lessons and equipment rentals**.

■ Watch the Sunset

The sunsets in Waikiki are **breathtaking**, with hues of orange, pink, and purple reflecting over the ocean. The best spots include **Queen's Surf Beach** or the **Hilton Hawaiian Village Lagoon**.

🍽 Dine at Oceanfront Restaurants

Enjoy fresh seafood, tropical cocktails, and Hawaiian cuisine at **Duke's Waikiki**, **House Without a Key**, or **Hula Grill**—all offering fantastic ocean views.

🚶 Stroll Along the Waikiki Promenade

Lined with **luxury shops, street performers, and cultural exhibits**, the promenade is a lively place to explore, especially in the evening.

🎵 Experience Nightlife & Live Music

From beachside bars to live Hawaiian music performances, Waikiki has a vibrant nightlife scene. Check out **Blue Note Hawaii** for jazz and **The Beach Bar** for tropical drinks with ocean views.

Summary

Waikiki Beach is the **heart of Oahu's tourism scene**, offering **world-famous surf, stunning sunsets, lively shopping areas, and rich cultural history**. Whether you're **learning to surf, enjoying a romantic beachfront dinner, or simply soaking in the island vibes**, Waikiki provides an unforgettable experience. Its combination of **natural beauty and urban energy** makes it a must-visit destination for anyone traveling to Oahu.

3.4 Hanauma Bay Nature Preserve

Short History

Hanauma Bay, located on the southeastern coast of Oahu, is a stunning marine embayment formed within a volcanic crater. The name "Hanauma" comes from the Hawaiian words *hana* (bay) and *uma* (curved), referencing its crescent shape. Historically, this bay was a **favorite fishing and recreational spot for Hawaiian royalty**.

In the mid-20th century, Hanauma Bay became a popular tourist destination, but decades of unregulated tourism led to environmental damage. In 1967, it was **declared a protected marine life conservation district**, and in 1990, conservation efforts were intensified, limiting the number of daily visitors. Today, Hanauma Bay is one of the most **well-preserved snorkeling destinations in Hawaii**, offering an unforgettable glimpse into Oahu's marine ecosystem.

Description

Hanauma Bay is renowned for its **crystal-clear waters, vibrant coral reefs, and abundant marine life**. The bay is home to **over 400 species of fish**, including the famous **Hawaiian state fish, the humuhumunukunukuāpua'a (reef triggerfish)**. Visitors often encounter **green sea turtles (honu), moray eels, and colorful parrotfish** while snorkeling.

The beach itself is a **pristine stretch of golden sand**, backed by lush, volcanic cliffs. Since it's a protected nature preserve, there are strict regulations in place to **minimize human impact and preserve the reef**. Visitors are required to **watch an educational video** before entering, emphasizing responsible snorkeling practices such as avoiding stepping on coral and not feeding fish.

Visitor Information

📍 Location

100 Hanauma Bay Road, Honolulu, HI 96825, USA

💰 Price

- **General Admission:** $25 per person (non-residents)
- **Hawaii Residents & Military:** Free with valid ID
- **Children (12 & under):** Free
- **Parking Fee:** $3 per vehicle
- **Snorkel Rental:** $20 per set

⏰ Opening Hours

- **Wednesday – Sunday:** 6:45 AM – 4:00 PM (last entry at 1:30 PM)
- **Closed Monday & Tuesday** (for reef conservation)

🌐 Website

www.honolulu.gov/hanaumabay

🔑 Key Features

- **Top Snorkeling Spot:** Calm, clear waters with abundant marine life
- **Educational Programs:** Mandatory conservation video before entry
- **Scenic Views:** Overlook provides breathtaking photo opportunities
- **Wildlife Encounters:** Frequent sightings of sea turtles and reef fish
- **Limited Daily Visitors:** Helps protect the fragile ecosystem

🔔 Visitor Services

- ✔ Snorkel Equipment Rental
- ✔ Lifeguard Stations
- ✔ Restrooms & Outdoor Showers
- ✔ Snack Bar & Picnic Areas
- ✔ Educational Marine Center

Things to Do at Hanauma Bay

🐢 Snorkeling

Hanauma Bay offers **some of the best snorkeling in Hawaii**, with calm, shallow waters ideal for beginners. For the best experience:

- Arrive early to avoid crowds and secure a good spot on the beach.
- Stick to designated snorkeling areas to protect the reef.
- Bring **reef-safe sunscreen** to minimize coral damage.

🚶 Explore the Scenic Overlook

Before heading down to the beach, stop by the **Hanauma Bay Lookout** for **breathtaking panoramic views** of the bay and Pacific Ocean.

🐢 Spot Green Sea Turtles

Honu (Hawaiian green sea turtles) are frequently seen **gliding gracefully through the water**. While it's tempting to get close, remember that touching or disturbing them is prohibited by law.

🎥 Learn at the Marine Education Center

The on-site **Marine Education Center** provides fascinating insights into the bay's ecology, including interactive exhibits about coral reef conservation and marine life.

Summary

Hanauma Bay Nature Preserve is a **must-visit destination for nature lovers and snorkeling enthusiasts**. With its **stunning underwater world, rich marine biodiversity, and strong conservation efforts**, it offers an unparalleled experience of Oahu's aquatic beauty. Visitors should plan ahead, **arrive early, respect conservation rules, and embrace the opportunity to explore one of Hawaii's most precious natural treasures**.

3.5 Iolani Palace

Short History

Iolani Palace, located in downtown Honolulu, is the only **royal palace in the United States** and a powerful symbol of Hawaii's monarchy. It was built in **1882 by King Kalākaua**, the last reigning king of Hawaii, as a grand residence that rivaled the palaces of European royalty. The palace was ahead of its time, featuring **electric lighting, indoor plumbing, and a telephone system before even the White House**.

After the overthrow of Queen Liliʻuokalani in 1893, the palace was used as government offices before being restored to its former glory in the 1970s. Today, it stands as a

National Historic Landmark, offering visitors a glimpse into Hawaii's royal past and cultural heritage.

Description

Iolani Palace is a **stunning example of Hawaiian Renaissance architecture**, blending Western influences with Hawaiian motifs. The **exquisite koa wood staircase, grand reception halls, elaborate throne room, and royal bedrooms** transport visitors to the era of Hawaii's monarchy.

One of the most moving parts of the tour is the **imprisonment room**, where Queen Liliʻuokalani was held under house arrest for nearly eight months after the Hawaiian monarchy was overthrown. Her handmade **"Queen's Quilt,"** stitched during her confinement, remains a poignant reminder of Hawaii's turbulent past.

Outside, the palace grounds feature the **Coronation Pavilion**, where Hawaiian monarchs were crowned, and **sacred royal burial sites**. The palace is not just a historical attraction—it is a **symbol of Hawaiian identity and resilience**.

Visitor Information

📍 Location

364 S King St, Honolulu, HI 96813, USA

💰 Price

- **Self-Guided Tour:** $25 per adult, $10 per child (5-12 years)
- **Docent-Led Tour:** $30 per adult, $12 per child
- **Hawaii Residents & Military Discounts Available**

🕐 Opening Hours

- **Tuesday – Saturday:** 9:00 AM – 4:00 PM
- **Closed Sundays, Mondays, and Major Holidays**

🌐 Website

iolanipalace.org

🔑 Key Features

- Only Royal Palace in the U.S.
- Authentic Restorations of the Throne Room & Royal Chambers

- ■ Artifacts from Hawaii's Last Monarchs
- ■ Interactive Museum & Guided Tours
- ■ Sacred Burial Grounds & Coronation Pavilion

🛎 Visitor Services

- ✔ Guided & Self-Guided Tours
- ✔ Gift Shop with Hawaiian Royal Memorabilia
- ✔ Wheelchair Accessibility
- ✔ Photography Permitted (No Flash Inside)
- ✔ Cultural Events & Educational Programs

Things to Do at Iolani Palace

🏛 Take a Guided Tour

A **docent-led tour** offers an in-depth look at the **lives of Hawaii's last monarchs**, their political struggles, and the overthrow of the Hawaiian Kingdom. For a more flexible experience, opt for a **self-guided audio tour**.

📜 Visit the Imprisonment Room

Step into the **sombre chamber where Queen Liliʻuokalani was held captive**, and see the **quilt she sewed while under house arrest**, a powerful symbol of her strength.

🎷 Experience the Throne Room & Grand Hall

Admire the **gold-trimmed throne room**, where Hawaiian royalty once hosted lavish events, and the **stunning koa wood staircase** leading to the upper chambers.

🎵 Explore the Royal Music Room

Discover the **musical legacy of King Kalākaua**, who introduced the world to hula performances and Hawaiian music.

🌳 Walk the Palace Grounds

Stroll through the **royal gardens**, see the **Coronation Pavilion**, and pay respects at the **sacred burial sites** of Hawaii's past rulers.

Summary

Iolani Palace is **more than just a historic site**—it is a **living testament to Hawaii's royal heritage and cultural resilience**. With its **opulent interiors, powerful history, and beautifully restored grounds**, the palace offers a unique window into Hawaii's past. **A visit here is essential for anyone looking to understand the true history of the Hawaiian Islands.**

3.6 Kualoa Ranch & Private Nature Reserve

Short History

Kualoa Ranch, located on Oahu's windward coast, is a **4,000-acre private nature reserve and working cattle ranch** with deep cultural and historical significance. Originally a sacred land for Hawaiian chiefs, it was later acquired by the Judd family in **1850**, who transformed it into a cattle ranch. Today, it is one of Hawaii's most famous attractions, known for its **breathtaking landscapes, adventure tours, and Hollywood movie locations**.

Kualoa is often called **"Hawaii's Jurassic Park"** because of its role in major films like *Jurassic Park, Jumanji, Godzilla,* and *Kong: Skull Island*. However, beyond the movie fame, it remains an important site for **Hawaiian agriculture, conservation, and eco-tourism**.

Description

Kualoa Ranch is divided into three main valleys:

- **Kualoa Valley (northern section)** – Famous for its stunning **mountain views, World War II bunkers, and Hollywood filming sites.**
- **Kaʻaʻawa Valley (central section)** – A dramatic green valley known for its **ATV and horseback riding trails, ancient Hawaiian sites, and scenic lookouts.**
- **Hakipuʻu Valley (southern section)** – Features the beautiful **Molii Fishpond, Secret Island Beach, and lush tropical forests.**

From **off-road jungle expeditions** to **kayaking and horseback riding**, Kualoa Ranch is an **adventurer's paradise** while also offering **family-friendly tours,** Hawaiian cultural experiences, and conservation programs.

Visitor Information

📍 Location

49-560 Kamehameha Hwy, Kaneohe, HI 96744, USA

💰 Price (Varies by Tour)

- **Jurassic Adventure Tour:** $144 per adult, $72 per child
- **ATV Raptor Tour:** $144 per adult (minimum age: 5)
- **Horseback Riding:** $104 per person (minimum age: 10)
- **Secret Island Beach Activities:** $54 per adult, $39 per child
- **Movie Sites & Ranch Tour:** $56 per adult, $40 per child

⏰ Opening Hours

- **Daily:** 8:00 AM – 5:30 PM
- **Reservations Required**

🌐 Website

www.kualoa.com

🔑 Key Features

▪ Jurassic Park & Hollywood Filming Locations
▪ ATV, Ziplining, & Horseback Riding Adventures

- Secret Island Beach with Kayaking & Paddleboarding
- Ancient Hawaiian Cultural Sites & Fishponds
- Sustainable Farming & Eco-Tourism Initiatives

🛎 Visitor Services

✔ Guided Tours & Adventure Packages
✔ On-Site Café & Gift Shop
✔ Restrooms & Changing Facilities
✔ Free Parking
✔ Eco-Conservation Programs

Things to Do at Kualoa Ranch

🦖 Jurassic Adventure Tour

Take a **scenic off-road journey through Ka'a'awa Valley**, where some of Hollywood's biggest blockbusters were filmed. Stop at **famous movie sets**, including the fallen log from *Jurassic Park*, Godzilla's footprint, and the massive Kong bones from *Kong: Skull Island*.

🐎 Horseback Riding & ATV Tours

Ride **through lush green valleys, past mountain ridges, and alongside scenic beaches**, taking in the breathtaking views of Kualoa's landscapes. Choose between **a gentle horseback ride or a thrilling ATV Raptor adventure**.

🏝 Secret Island Beach Activities

Relax or explore at **Kualoa's private beach**, featuring **kayaking, paddleboarding, beach volleyball, and hammocks**. The peaceful **Molii Fishpond**, a 800-year-old Hawaiian aquaculture site, is also nearby.

🌺 Hawaiian Cultural Experiences

Learn about **Hawaiian farming, fishing, and ancient traditions** on the **Malama Experience Tour**, where you'll visit the **sacred fishponds and taro patches** that have sustained native Hawaiians for centuries.

🌿 Zipline Through the Rainforest

Glide through **seven exciting zipline courses**, passing over **streams, tropical forests, and historical sites** in the lush Hakipu'u Valley.

Summary

Kualoa Ranch is **one of Oahu's most breathtaking and adventure-filled destinations**, offering a mix of **outdoor excitement, cultural experiences, and cinematic history**. Whether you're an adrenaline junkie, a history enthusiast, or just looking for scenic beauty, **this legendary ranch is a must-visit**.

3.7 Byodo-In Temple

Short History

The **Byodo-In Temple**, nestled at the foot of the **Ko'olau Mountains** in the **Valley of the Temples Memorial Park**, is a **non-denominational Buddhist temple** that honors Japanese culture and spiritual heritage in Hawaii. This stunning temple is a **replica of the 950-year-old Byodo-In Temple in Uji, Japan**, a UNESCO World Heritage Site.

Built in **1968** to commemorate the **100th anniversary of the first Japanese immigrants to Hawaii**, the temple serves as a place of **peace, reflection, and meditation** rather than an active Buddhist temple. Visitors from around the world come to experience its **tranquil gardens, koi ponds, and breathtaking architecture**, making it one of **Oahu's most serene hidden gems**.

Description

The Byodo-In Temple is **a masterpiece of Japanese architecture**, featuring a **graceful curved roof, intricate woodwork, and a towering golden Buddha statue** inside the main hall. The temple is surrounded by **lush gardens, koi-filled reflecting ponds, and a large meditation pavilion**, making it a **perfect escape from Oahu's busier attractions**.

As you step through the entrance, you'll pass under a **traditional torii gate**, symbolizing the transition into a sacred space. A **large three-ton peace bell, known as the bon-sho,** is located near the entrance—visitors are encouraged to **ring it before entering** as a sign of **respect, good luck, and clearing the mind of negative thoughts**.

Inside, the main hall houses **a 9-foot tall golden Amida Buddha statue**, carefully crafted with **gold leaf and lacquer**, symbolizing infinite compassion and wisdom. The temple grounds also feature **small meditation areas, a teahouse, and vibrant peacocks roaming freely**.

Visitor Information

📍 Location

47-200 Kahekili Hwy, Kaneohe, HI 96744, USA

💰 Price

- **Adults:** $5
- **Seniors (65+):** $4
- **Children (2-12 years):** $2
- **Infants (under 2):** Free

🕐 Opening Hours

- **Daily:** 8:30 AM – 5:00 PM

🌐 Website

www.byodo-in.com

🔑 **Key Features**

▪ Authentic Japanese Buddhist Temple
▪ 9-Foot Tall Golden Buddha Statue
▪ Serene Meditation Gardens & Walking Paths
▪ Koi Fish Ponds & Waterfalls
▪ 3-Ton Sacred Peace Bell (Bon-sho)
▪ Wild Peacocks & Black Swans

🔔 **Visitor Services**

✔ Gift Shop & Tea House
✔ Benches & Shaded Rest Areas
✔ On-Site Parking
✔ Photography Friendly (No Drones Allowed)
✔ Accessible Pathways for Wheelchairs

Things to Do at Byodo-In Temple

🔔 **Ring the Peace Bell**

Before entering the temple, **ring the massive bon-sho (sacred bell)** to bring **peace and harmony** to your mind. The sound resonates through the valley, creating a calming effect.

🙏 **Meditate & Reflect**

Sit quietly inside the temple or find a spot in the **gardens or meditation pavilion** to soak in the tranquil surroundings. Many visitors describe the **peaceful energy** here as **deeply spiritual and rejuvenating.**

🌿 **Stroll Through the Zen Gardens**

Explore the **lush Japanese gardens**, featuring **miniature waterfalls, vibrant koi fish swimming in tranquil ponds, and beautifully manicured bonsai trees**.

🌳 **Spot Wild Peacocks & Black Swans**

The temple grounds are home to **free-roaming peacocks, black swans, and turtles**, adding to the mystical and serene atmosphere.

📷 **Capture Stunning Photos**

The temple's **vivid red color, set against the emerald-green Koʻolau Mountains,** makes for breathtaking photographs.

🍎 Visit the Gift Shop & Tea House

Enjoy **traditional Japanese tea, incense, and unique souvenirs** at the small on-site shop.

Summary

The **Byodo-In Temple** is one of Oahu's most **peaceful and picturesque attractions**, offering a **glimpse into Japanese spirituality and architecture**. Whether you're looking for **a quiet retreat, a cultural experience, or simply a beautiful place to explore**, this hidden gem is **a must-visit destination**.

Chapter 4. Best Beaches in Oahu

4.1 Lanikai Beach

A Brief History & Overview

Lanikai Beach, meaning **"Heavenly Sea"** in Hawaiian, is often ranked among the **most beautiful beaches in the world**. Located in the town of **Kailua on Oahu's windward coast**, this small but stunning beach is famous for its **soft, powdery white sand, crystal-clear turquoise waters, and breathtaking views of the Mokulua Islands ("Mokes")**.

Unlike many of Oahu's other famous beaches, Lanikai is **not a state park** and has no official public facilities, making it feel like a secluded paradise. Over the years, it has been a favorite spot for **locals, celebrities, and travelers seeking a quiet escape** from the busier beaches like Waikiki.

Lanikai Beach is **perfect for swimming, kayaking, stand-up paddleboarding, and sunrise viewing**, as the **calm waters and offshore reef** make it one of the safest swimming beaches on the island.

Location & Accessibility

📍 **Location:** Mokulua Drive, Kailua, HI 96734, USA
💰 **Entrance Fee:** Free
🌐 **Website:** Go Hawaii – Lanikai Beach
🕐 **Opening Hours:** Open 24/7

How to Get There:

- 🚗 **By Car:** About **30 minutes from Waikiki**, but parking is limited to nearby residential streets.
- 🚌 **By Public Transport:** TheBus **Route 67** from Honolulu to Kailua, then walk or bike to Lanikai.
- 🚲 **By Bike:** Rent a bike in **Kailua Town** and enjoy the scenic ride to the beach.

Key Features & Activities

🌊 Calm, Crystal-Clear Waters

- Protected by an **offshore reef**, Lanikai's waters are **calm year-round**, making it ideal for **swimming**.
- **No strong currents** compared to North Shore beaches, making it **family-friendly**.

🌴 Stunning Views of the Mokulua Islands ("The Mokes")

- The **two small offshore islands** create a **picture-perfect backdrop**, especially at sunrise.
- The islands are part of a seabird sanctuary, and kayaking there is a popular activity.

🛶 Kayaking & Stand-Up Paddleboarding

- Calm conditions make **kayaking to the Mokulua Islands** an unforgettable adventure.
- Kayak rentals are available in **Kailua Town**, about a 5-minute drive away.

🌄 One of Oahu's Best Sunrise Spots

- Facing east, Lanikai offers **breathtaking sunrise views** over the Pacific.
- Many visitors and photographers arrive early to capture the **pastel-colored skies**.

🪧 White Sand Beach with a Secluded Feel

- Unlike Waikiki, Lanikai has **no hotels, large crowds, or commercial activity**, offering a peaceful retreat.

🐠 Snorkeling Opportunities

- The **shallow coral reefs** provide a home for tropical fish and sea turtles.
- Best snorkeling is near the rocky areas along the shore.

Visitor Services & Amenities

🚻 **Facilities: None** (No restrooms, showers, or lifeguards).
🅿️ **Parking: Street parking only** (Be respectful of local residents).
🛶 **Kayak Rentals:** Available in **Kailua Town** (a short drive or bike ride away).
🍽️ **Nearby Food Options:** Kailua Town has local cafes, smoothie shops, and restaurants.

Best Time to Visit

- 🌅 **For Sunrises: Early morning** (best before 7 AM).
- 🏊 **For Swimming & Snorkeling:** Year-round, but mornings offer the calmest waters.
- 🛶 **For Kayaking: Late morning or early afternoon** for the best conditions.

Summary

Lanikai Beach is a **true Hawaiian paradise**, offering a **secluded, tranquil setting with powdery white sand and clear blue waters**. Whether you want to **swim, kayak, watch the sunrise, or simply relax**, Lanikai is an unforgettable experience. Due to its lack of facilities and limited parking, it's best to **plan ahead and arrive early** to fully enjoy this breathtaking destination.

4.2 Sunset Beach

A Brief History & Overview

Sunset Beach is one of **Oahu's most legendary beaches**, located on the famous **North Shore**. Known for its **massive winter waves, golden sands, and picturesque sunsets**, the beach has long been a gathering spot for surfers, photographers, and beach lovers.

Historically, Sunset Beach gained prominence in the **1960s and 70s**, when it became one of the main locations for **professional surfing competitions**. It remains a key stop in the **Vans Triple Crown of Surfing**, a prestigious event showcasing the world's best surfers. In the **summer months**, when the waters are calmer, Sunset Beach transforms into a peaceful retreat perfect for **swimming, snorkeling, and beachcombing**.

With its **breathtaking coastal views, vibrant surf culture, and golden stretches of sand**, Sunset Beach is a **must-visit destination** in Oahu.

Location & Accessibility

- **Location:** Kamehameha Highway, Pupukea, HI 96712, USA
- **Entrance Fee:** Free
- **Website:** Hawaii State Parks
- **Opening Hours:** Open 24/7

How to Get There:

- 🚗 **By Car:** Easily accessible via **Kamehameha Highway (Route 83)**, approximately **1 hour from Waikiki**. Free roadside parking is available but fills up fast.
- 🚌 **By Public Transport:** TheBus **Route 60** from Honolulu or Haleiwa stops near Sunset Beach.
- 🚲 **By Bike:** A scenic bike path runs along the North Shore, making cycling an option for nearby visitors.

Key Features & Activities

🌊 Big Wave Surfing (Winter Months - November to February)

- Sunset Beach is part of **Oahu's "Seven Mile Miracle"**, a stretch of world-famous surf breaks.
- **Waves reach 15–30 feet**, making it a top location for professional surfing competitions.
- Home to **Vans Triple Crown of Surfing**, attracting top surfers worldwide.
- Not suitable for beginner surfers or casual swimmers due to **strong rip currents**.

🏖️ Swimming & Snorkeling (Summer Months - May to September)

- In summer, the waters **calm down**, creating perfect conditions for **snorkeling and swimming**.
- The **clear blue waters** reveal tropical fish and sea turtles near the reef.
- **Caution:** Watch for occasional strong currents, and always check ocean conditions before entering.

🌅 Stunning Sunsets

- Sunset Beach lives up to its name with **spectacular sunset views**.
- The horizon transforms into **vibrant shades of orange, pink, and purple**, creating a picture-perfect moment.

🚶 Beach Walks & Picnicking

- The **two-mile-long stretch of sand** is ideal for **walking, jogging, or relaxing with a picnic**.
- The beach is **less crowded** than Waikiki, offering a more peaceful atmosphere.

Visitor Services & Amenities

⭕ **Lifeguards:** On duty daily (essential for safety during high surf seasons).
▪ **Facilities:** Public restrooms and outdoor showers available.
▪ **Parking:** Free parking lot and roadside parking (fills up quickly).
🍽 **Nearby Food Options:** Food trucks and local restaurants along Kamehameha Highway.
🏄 **Surf Schools & Rentals:** Available in nearby Haleiwa and Turtle Bay Resort.

Best Time to Visit

- 🏄 **For Surfing: November–February** (best for experienced surfers).
- 🌊 **For Swimming & Snorkeling: May–September** (calmer waters).
- ▪ **For Sunsets:** Year-round, but **clear-sky evenings** provide the best views.

Summary

Sunset Beach is an **iconic North Shore destination**, offering **thrilling surf competitions in winter and peaceful beach days in summer**. Whether you come for the **big waves, relaxing swims, or breathtaking sunsets**, this beach is a must-visit for anyone exploring Oahu.

4.3 Kailua Beach Park

A Brief History & Overview

Kailua Beach Park, located on Oahu's **windward coast**, is often considered one of the **best beaches in Hawaii**. Just a mile away from the famous Lanikai Beach, this **2.5-mile stretch of soft, white sand** offers stunning turquoise waters, making it a top destination for **swimming, kayaking, windsurfing, and picnicking**.

Historically, the Kailua area was home to Hawaiian royalty, who valued its **gentle waters, lush surroundings, and trade winds**. Today, it remains a favorite among both locals and tourists, offering **modern amenities, ample parking, and a more accessible alternative to Lanikai Beach**.

Unlike many other Oahu beaches, Kailua Beach is **not lined with hotels or resorts**, maintaining a laid-back, community feel. Its calm yet breezy conditions make it a **world-renowned spot for windsurfing and kiteboarding**, attracting professionals and beginners alike.

Location & Accessibility

- **Location:** 526 Kawailoa Rd, Kailua, HI 96734, USA
- **Entrance Fee:** Free
- **Website:** Go Hawaii – Kailua Beach Park
- **Opening Hours:** 5:00 AM – 10:00 PM

How to Get There:

- 🚗 **By Car:** A **30-minute drive from Waikiki**, with **ample free parking** available.
- 🚌 **By Public Transport:** TheBus **Route 67** from Honolulu to Kailua.
- 🚲 **By Bike:** Rent a bike in **Kailua Town** and enjoy a scenic ride to the beach.

Key Features & Activities

🌊 **Calm, Clear Waters with Soft White Sand**

- Shallow, **gentle waves make it great for swimming**, especially for families.
- The **sand is soft and clean**, perfect for sunbathing and relaxing.

🛶 **Kayaking to the Mokulua Islands & Popoi'a Island (Flat Island)**

- **Kayak rentals are available nearby**, and paddling to the islands is a popular activity.
- **Mokulua Islands ("The Mokes")** are visible offshore, offering an adventurous kayaking trip.
- **Flat Island (Popoi'a)** is a small, rocky island just offshore, ideal for a short kayak excursion.

🏄 **World-Class Windsurfing & Kiteboarding**

- Kailua Beach is one of the **best windsurfing and kiteboarding spots in the world**.
- Consistent **trade winds** make it perfect for beginners and pros alike.

🐢 **Snorkeling & Marine Life**

- The **clear waters** near the reefs provide great visibility for spotting tropical fish and sea turtles.
- Best snorkeling areas are **closer to Lanikai Beach**.

🌴 **Large, Family-Friendly Beach Park**

- Unlike Lanikai, Kailua Beach has **plenty of space** for families, with grassy areas and picnic tables.

Visitor Services & Amenities

■ **Facilities:** Restrooms, showers, picnic tables, BBQ grills.
● **Lifeguards on Duty:** Yes.
■ **Parking:** Free and **plentiful** (compared to Lanikai Beach).
🛶 **Equipment Rentals:** Kayaks, stand-up paddleboards, and windsurfing gear available in Kailua Town.
🍴 **Nearby Food Options:**

- **Buzz's Original Steakhouse** – Local favorite for seafood & Hawaiian cuisine.
- **Kalapawai Market** – Perfect for sandwiches, snacks, and coffee.

Best Time to Visit

- 🌅 **For Sunrise Views:** Early morning (before 7 AM).
- 🏖 **For Swimming & Relaxation:** Year-round, but mornings offer the calmest conditions.
- 🛶 **For Kayaking & Windsurfing: Mid-morning to early afternoon**, when trade winds are steady but manageable.

Summary

Kailua Beach Park is the **perfect balance of beauty, accessibility, and activities**. Whether you want to **swim, kayak, windsurf, or just relax on the soft sand**, it offers something for everyone. With **modern amenities, plenty of parking, and nearby restaurants**, it's a **top choice for families, adventure-seekers, and beach lovers**.

4.4 Waimea Bay

A Brief History & Overview

Waimea Bay, located on Oahu's **North Shore**, is one of the most **legendary surf spots in the world**. Known for its **towering winter waves**, sometimes reaching up to **40 feet**, this bay has been a focal point of **big-wave surfing since the 1950s**. In contrast, during the summer months, the bay transforms into a **calm, turquoise oasis** perfect for swimming, snorkeling, and cliff jumping.

Historically, Waimea Bay was a **sacred place** for Native Hawaiians, serving as a significant settlement and religious site. Nearby, Waimea Valley was home to **Hawaiian high priests** (kahuna), and remnants of ancient temples (heiau) still exist. Today, the bay is part of **Pūpūkea Marine Life Conservation District**, ensuring the protection of its vibrant marine ecosystem.

Location & Accessibility

- **Location:** Kamehameha Hwy, Haleiwa, HI 96712, USA
- **Entrance Fee:** Free
- **Website:** Hawaii State Parks – Waimea Bay
- **Opening Hours:** 7:00 AM – 7:00 PM

How to Get There:

- **By Car:** A **one-hour drive from Waikiki** along the scenic Kamehameha Highway. Limited parking available.
- **By Public Transport:** TheBus **Route 60** from Honolulu to the North Shore.
- **By Bike:** Possible from Haleiwa, but be prepared for some uphill sections.

Key Features & Activities

Big-Wave Surfing (Winter Only)

- One of the most famous **big-wave surf spots in the world**.
- Waves **reach up to 40 feet** in peak winter months (November – February).
- Home to the **Eddie Aikau Big Wave Invitational**, held only when waves exceed **30 feet**.

🐚 Calm Waters & Swimming (Summer Only)

- During the summer (May – September), the bay becomes **crystal-clear and tranquil**, perfect for swimming.
- **No waves, minimal currents**, and shallow waters near the shore.

🐠 Snorkeling & Marine Life Viewing

- Part of the **Pūpūkea Marine Conservation District**, making it a great spot for marine biodiversity.
- Frequent sightings of **colorful tropical fish, sea turtles, and Hawaiian monk seals**.

🪂 Cliff Jumping (Famous Rock at Waimea Bay)

- A **25-foot rock formation** on the left side of the bay attracts adventurous cliff jumpers.
- Safe in summer, but **dangerous during winter due to strong waves**.

📷 Sunset Views & Photography

- **One of the best sunset spots** on Oahu, offering stunning golden-hour views.
- Excellent for **photography enthusiasts**, especially during surf season.

visitor services & amenities

🏛 **Facilities:** Restrooms, showers, picnic tables.
🛑 **Lifeguards on Duty:** Yes (Highly important during winter surf season).
🅿 **Parking: Very limited**, arrive early or park in nearby areas and walk.
🍽 **Nearby Food Options:**

- **Haleiwa Town** (10 minutes away) offers great local food, including shrimp trucks.
- **Waimea Valley Snack Bar** – Quick bites and refreshments.

Best Time to Visit

- 🏄 **For Surf Watching: November – February**, when big waves are at their peak.
- 🐚 **For Swimming & Snorkeling: May – September**, when the waters are calm and clear.
- 📷 **For Sunsets & Cliff Jumping:** Late afternoon to early evening.

Summary

Waimea Bay is an **iconic destination** that offers **two completely different experiences** depending on the season. In the winter, it's a **spectacular surf mecca**, attracting professionals and surf enthusiasts from around the world. In the summer, it's a **serene paradise** with crystal-clear waters, perfect for swimming, snorkeling, and cliff jumping. With its **rich history, dramatic landscapes, and world-class waves**, Waimea Bay is an absolute must-visit for any Oahu traveler.

4.5 Makapuʻu Beach

A Brief History & Overview

Makapuʻu Beach, located on Oahu's **southeastern coast**, is a strikingly beautiful beach known for its **rugged cliffs, turquoise waters, and powerful shorebreak waves**. The beach sits beneath the **famous Makapuʻu Lighthouse**, offering breathtaking views of the Pacific Ocean and nearby **Rabbit Island (Mānana Island)**.

Historically, the area around Makapuʻu was significant to Native Hawaiians, who used the cliffs and offshore waters for **fishing and navigation**. The beach's name, "Makapuʻu," means **"bulging eye"** in Hawaiian, likely referring to a volcanic feature in the area. Today, it's a **favorite spot for bodyboarders and adventure seekers**, offering a dramatic landscape unlike any other on Oahu.

Location & Accessibility

- 📍 **Location:** Kalanianaʻole Hwy, Waimānalo, HI 96795, USA
- 💰 **Entrance Fee:** Free
- 🌐 **Website:** [Hawaii State Parks – Makapuʻu](#)
- 🕐 **Opening Hours:** Open 24/7, but best visited during daylight hours.

How to Get There:

- 🚗 **By Car:** A **40-minute drive from Waikiki**, with scenic ocean views along the way.
- 🚌 **By Public Transport:** TheBus **Route 23** from Waikiki stops nearby.
- 🚶 **By Foot:** A short walk from the **Makapuʻu Lighthouse Trailhead**.

Key Features & Activities

🌊 **Powerful Shorebreak Waves (For Experienced Bodyboarders Only)**

- **One of Oahu's top bodyboarding beaches**, with consistent waves.

- **Not recommended for inexperienced swimmers** due to strong currents.
- Frequented by local **bodyboarders and bodysurfers**.

🐚 Tide Pools & Marine Life Viewing

- Just beyond the main beach, **Makapuʻu tide pools** offer a unique spot for exploring small marine creatures.
- **Best visited during low tide** for safe access.

■ Stunning Scenery & Photography

- The beach is framed by **black volcanic rock cliffs**, creating a **picturesque contrast with the blue ocean**.
- Great views of **Rabbit Island (Mānana Island)** and **Kaohikaipu Island**.

🚶 Proximity to Makapuʻu Lighthouse Trail

- **A short drive or walk** from the famous **Makapuʻu Point Lighthouse Trail**, offering spectacular panoramic views.
- **Ideal for combining a beach visit with a scenic hike**.

Visitor Services & Amenities

■ **Facilities:** Restrooms and outdoor showers available.
⬢ **Lifeguards on Duty:** Yes, but swimmers should still be cautious.
■ **Parking:** Free parking lot available, but it can fill up quickly on weekends.
⬢ **Nearby Food Options:**

- **Waimānalo Town** (a short drive away) offers **local Hawaiian plate lunches and fresh fruit stands**.
- **Shrimp trucks and food trucks** often park nearby.

Best Time to Visit

- 🏄 **For Bodyboarding: Year-round**, but waves are strongest in the **winter months (November – April)**.
- 📷 **For Photography & Sightseeing: Early morning or sunset** for the best lighting.
- 🐚 **For Exploring Tide Pools: Low tide**, when the pools are more accessible.

Summary

Makapuʻu Beach is a **stunning, rugged destination** known for its **strong shorebreak waves, dramatic cliffs, and crystal-clear waters**. While it's a paradise for **experienced bodyboarders and adventurers**, swimmers should **exercise caution due to strong currents**. Its proximity to **Makapuʻu Lighthouse Trail** makes it a **perfect stop for travelers looking to combine beach time with scenic hiking**. Whether you're here for the **views, bodyboarding, or tide pools**, Makapuʻu Beach is a **must-visit on Oahu's southeastern coast**.

4.6 Sandy Beach

A Brief History & Overview

Sandy Beach, located on Oahu's **southeastern shore**, is famous for its **powerful shorebreak waves, golden sand, and thrilling bodyboarding conditions**. Known locally as **"Breakneck Beach"**, this stretch of coastline is **notoriously dangerous for inexperienced swimmers** due to its strong waves and rip currents.

The area around Sandy Beach has long been used by **Native Hawaiians for fishing and ocean navigation**, and its **exposed location** makes it one of the best places to experience the **raw power of the Pacific Ocean**. The beach is a **favorite spot among local bodyboarders and surfers**, as well as a **scenic getaway for visitors** looking to enjoy Oahu's rugged coastline.

Location & Accessibility

- 📍 **Location:** Kalanianaʻole Hwy, Honolulu, HI 96825, USA
- 💰 **Entrance Fee:** Free
- 🌐 **Website:** Hawaii State Parks – Sandy Beach
- 🕐 **Opening Hours:** Open 24/7, but best visited during daylight hours.

How to Get There:

- 🚗 **By Car:** A **35-minute drive from Waikiki**, following the scenic **Kalanianaʻole Highway** past Hanauma Bay.
- 🚌 **By Public Transport:** TheBus **Route 22 or 23** from Waikiki stops nearby.
- 🚴 **By Bike:** The **coastal road** is popular for cycling, though the ride can be challenging.

Key Features & Activities

🌊 **World-Famous Bodyboarding & Bodysurfing**

- **Considered one of the best bodyboarding beaches in Hawaii** due to its powerful shorebreak.
- **Caution: Not recommended for beginners**—waves break directly onto the shore, making it dangerous for those unfamiliar with strong surf.

🌴 **Scenic Views & Photography**

- Surrounded by **volcanic rock formations and dramatic cliffs**, Sandy Beach offers **stunning ocean views**.
- **Sunrises are spectacular**, making it a favorite spot for **photographers and early risers**.

🐚 **Marine Life Spotting & Nearby Tide Pools**

- While the waves are too strong for swimming, **nearby tide pools** offer calmer waters for spotting **small fish and crabs**.
- Look out for **monk seals and sea turtles** that occasionally rest on the beach.

🌅 **Sunset & Stargazing**

- While not as famous as Sunset Beach, **Sandy Beach's location away from the city lights** makes it a great place for **stargazing on clear nights**.

Visitor Services & Amenities

🚻 **Facilities:** Restrooms and outdoor showers available.
🛟 **Lifeguards on Duty:** Yes—lifeguards are stationed here daily due to strong waves.
🅿️ **Parking:** Free parking lot available, but it fills up quickly on weekends.
🍽️ **Nearby Food Options:**

- **Lunch trucks** and food stalls often stop nearby, selling **local Hawaiian dishes**.
- **Waimānalo and Hawaii Kai** (a short drive away) have restaurants and convenience stores.

Best Time to Visit

- 🏄 **For Bodyboarding & Surfing: Year-round**, but waves are strongest in the **summer months (May – September)**.

- 📷 **For Photography & Sightseeing: Early morning (sunrise) or late afternoon** for the best lighting.
- 🚶 **For Relaxing & Beach Walks: Weekdays** are less crowded than weekends.

Safety Tips

⚠️ **Warning: Strong Shorebreak!**

- **Not a swimming beach**—waves crash directly onto the shore, making it extremely dangerous for inexperienced swimmers.
- If you're new to bodyboarding, watch the **locals** before entering the water.

☀️ **Sun Protection:**

- Sandy Beach has **no shade**, so bring sunscreen, a hat, and plenty of water.

🐚 **Be Cautious Around Marine Life:**

- Occasionally, **jellyfish and sea urchins** can be found in the tide pools—watch where you step.

Summary

Sandy Beach is a **stunning but extreme beach**, best known for its **thrilling bodyboarding waves, scenic ocean views, and rugged beauty**. While **not ideal for swimming**, it's a **must-visit spot for adventure seekers, photographers, and those looking to experience Oahu's powerful coastline**. Whether you're here to **watch the pros take on the waves, snap incredible sunrise photos, or enjoy a peaceful beach walk**, Sandy Beach is an **iconic destination that showcases Hawaii's untamed natural beauty**.

Chapter 5. Outdoor Adventures and Activities

5.1 Hiking Trails: Koko Crater, Manoa Falls, and Lanikai Pillbox Trail

Oahu is home to some of **Hawaii's most scenic and diverse hiking trails**, ranging from **challenging volcanic ascents** to **gentle rainforest walks**. Whether you're looking for a strenuous workout, a lush jungle adventure, or an iconic sunrise view, these three **must-visit trails—Koko Crater, Manoa Falls, and Lanikai Pillbox**—offer unforgettable outdoor experiences.

Koko Crater Railway Trail (Koko Head Stairs)

Historical Background

The **Koko Crater Railway Trail**, often called the **Koko Head Stairs**, is a **remnant of World War II**, where the U.S. military installed a **tramway** to transport **troops and supplies** to bunkers at the summit. The **railroad ties** have since become **1,048 grueling steps**, making this hike both a **historical landmark** and a **fitness challenge**.

Trail Description & Conditions

- **Difficulty Level: Very Difficult** (Steep incline, fully exposed to the sun)
- **Distance: 1.8 miles round trip**
- **Elevation Gain: 1,208 feet**
- **Time to Complete: 1.5 to 2.5 hours round trip**

The climb **begins immediately** with a steep incline, and as you ascend, the steps become **more spaced out** and **uneven**, making it progressively harder. There is a **"bridge section"** where the steps are suspended over a **gap in the trail**—many hikers choose to walk alongside it instead.

At the summit, you'll find **old military bunkers** and one of the most **spectacular panoramic views** on Oahu, including **Hanauma Bay, Diamond Head, and the Pacific Ocean** stretching into the horizon.

Best Time to Hike

☀ **Sunrise (5:30 AM - 7:00 AM)** – Cooler temperatures, breathtaking golden-hour lighting.

🌄 **Late Afternoon (4:00 PM - 6:00 PM)** – Avoids peak heat, offers stunning sunset views.

Photography & Viewpoints

📷 **Best Spots for Photos:**

- **Halfway up** – Offers a dramatic perspective of the railway stretching below.
- **Summit bunkers** – Capture **unobstructed panoramic landscapes**.
- **Sunrise Shots** – The sky transforms with deep **orange, pink, and purple hues** over the coastline.

Wildlife & Flora

🦎 **Hawaiian Geckos** – Often spotted basking on rocks.
🌵 **Dryland Shrubs & Cacti** – Unique to Oahu's leeward volcanic slopes.

Tips for Hikers

💧 **Bring at least 1 liter of water** – There's no shade or water stations.
👟 **Wear sturdy hiking shoes** – The **uneven wooden steps** require good traction.
🧴 **Use sunscreen & a hat** – The entire trail is **exposed to the sun**.

■ **Take breaks every 200 steps** – Many hikers stop to catch their breath and enjoy the view.

Manoa Falls Trail

Historical Background

Located in **the lush Manoa Valley**, this **family-friendly hike** leads to a **150-foot waterfall** that **flows year-round**. The area has a long history as a **sacred Hawaiian site**, known for its **legends of Night Marchers (ghostly warriors)** and its deep connection to native Hawaiian **water spirits (moʻo)**.

It has also been used as a **filming location** for **Jurassic Park** and **Lost**, making it a favorite for movie lovers.

Trail Description & Conditions

- Difficulty Level: Easy to Moderate
- Distance: 1.7 miles round trip
- Elevation Gain: 633 feet
- Time to Complete: 1 to 1.5 hours round trip

The trail **begins with a gradual incline** through a **dense bamboo forest** before transitioning into a **canopy of towering banyan and eucalyptus trees**. The **path can be muddy and slippery** after rain, but it's well-maintained and easy to follow.

At the end, you'll reach **Manoa Falls**, cascading over a **basalt rock face**, surrounded by **ferns, vines, and tropical flowers**.

Best Time to Hike

🌿 **Morning (7:00 AM - 10:00 AM)** – Cooler and **less crowded**.

☔ **After Light Rain** – The waterfall becomes more powerful, but avoid heavy downpours.

Photography & Viewpoints

📷 **Best Spots for Photos:**

- **Bamboo Groves** – Creates a dramatic, **tunnel-like atmosphere**.
- **Manoa Falls Base** – Stunning **lush backdrop** for photos.
- **Jungle Canopy** – Captures the ethereal **"rainforest mist"** effect.

Wildlife & Flora

🦉 **Hawaiian Honeycreepers** – Colorful birds frequently spotted here.
🌿 **Orchids & Ginger Plants** – Add bursts of color along the trail.

Tips for Hikers

⬛ **Wear waterproof hiking shoes** – The trail can get **muddy**.
⬛ **Bring insect repellent** – Mosquitoes are common in the valley.
⬛ **Stay on the trail** – **Climbing on rocks near the waterfall is prohibited** for safety reasons.

Lanikai Pillbox Trail (Kaiwa Ridge Trail)

Historical Background

Built in the **1940s during World War II**, the **pillboxes** on this ridge were used as **military observation posts** to monitor **enemy aircraft and ships**. Today, they serve as **one of the best sunrise viewpoints on Oahu**.

Trail Description & Conditions

- Difficulty Level: Moderate
- Distance: 1.6 miles round trip
- Elevation Gain: 600 feet
- Time to Complete: 1 to 1.5 hours round trip

The trail starts with a **steep dirt path** that quickly ascends the ridge. Along the way, you'll have **expansive views of Kailua Beach, Lanikai Beach, and the Mokulua Islands**. There are **two main pillboxes**, both painted in **colorful graffiti**, making them **popular photo spots**.

Best Time to Hike

⬛ **Sunrise (5:45 AM - 7:00 AM)** – The **most breathtaking view**, with pink and orange hues.
🌼 **Early Morning (Before 9:00 AM)** – Less crowded, cooler temperatures.

Photography & Viewpoints

📷 **Best Spots for Photos:**

- **First Pillbox** – Overlooks **Lanikai Beach and Mokulua Islands**.

- **Second Pillbox** – Higher vantage point for **a wide panorama of the Windward Coast**.
- **Sunrise Shots** – Silhouetted **pillboxes against a golden sky**.

Wildlife & Flora

🦋 **Hawaiian Butterflies** – Often seen near wildflowers along the trail.
🌴 **Ironwood & Kiawe Trees** – Hardy plants adapted to dry coastal environments.

Tips for Hikers

▪ **Wear grippy shoes** – Some sections are **steep and loose with dirt**.
▪ **Arrive early for parking** – Limited spots in **residential Lanikai**.
▪ **Pack a headlamp** – Essential if hiking for **sunrise**.

Summary

- **Koko Crater** – A **steep WWII railway hike** with **panoramic island views**.
- **Manoa Falls** – A **rainforest trek** leading to a **stunning waterfall**.
- **Lanikai Pillbox** – A **short sunrise hike** with **incredible ocean vistas**.

Each trail offers **unique scenery, history, and challenges**, making them **must-experience hikes** for any Oahu traveler.

I'll provide a **detailed** breakdown of **Hanauma Bay and Shark's Cove**, including **history, location, entrance fees, best times to visit, marine life, safety tips, and insider recommendations** for **snorkeling and diving** in these incredible spots.

5.2 Snorkeling and Diving Spots: Hanauma Bay and Shark's Cove

Oahu is **world-famous** for its **crystal-clear waters, vibrant coral reefs, and diverse marine life**, making it a top destination for snorkeling and diving. Two of the island's most **spectacular underwater locations** are **Hanauma Bay** and **Shark's Cove**—each offering unique marine ecosystems, breathtaking visibility, and unforgettable underwater encounters.

Hanauma Bay Nature Preserve

Historical Background

Hanauma Bay, a **stunning crescent-shaped bay**, was formed within a **volcanic tuff ring** over **32,000 years ago**. Historically, it was a **fishing site for Hawaiian royalty** and remains one of Hawaii's most **protected marine ecosystems** today. Due to past overuse, it was **designated a nature preserve in 1967**, implementing **strict conservation rules** to protect its **delicate coral reefs and marine species**.

Location & Accessibility

- 📍 **Address:** 7455 Kalaniana'ole Hwy, Honolulu, HI 96825
- 🗺️ **Location:** Southeast Oahu, about **30 minutes from Waikiki**
- 🚗 **Parking:** Limited parking available (**$3 per vehicle**); fills up early

Entrance Fees & Reservations

- 💲 **General Admission:** $25 per person (**Hawaii residents enter free**)
- 📅 **Reservations Required:** Book online in advance at [Hanauma Bay Website](#)
- 📆 **Closed Mondays & Tuesdays** for reef conservation

Opening Hours

- ⏰ **Wednesday – Sunday:** 6:45 AM – 4:00 PM (**Last entry at 1:30 PM**)

Best Time to Visit

- ☀️ **Early Morning (Before 9 AM)** – Fewer crowds, better visibility
- 🌙 **Midweek (Wednesday or Thursday)** – Avoids weekend rush

Snorkeling Experience & Marine Life

Hanauma Bay is known for its **calm, shallow waters** and **abundant marine life**, making it perfect for **beginners and families**. The **inner reef** is ideal for novice snorkelers, while the **outer reef** (deeper waters) offers more advanced snorkeling and occasional **green sea turtle (honu) sightings**.

🐟 **Common Marine Species:**

- **Hawaiian Green Sea Turtles** – Often seen resting on the reef
- **Humuhumunukunukuapua'a (Hawaii's State Fish)** – Vibrant triggerfish
- **Parrotfish** – Recognizable by their bright colors and beak-like mouths
- **Eels & Octopuses** – Hiding in rocky crevices

🌿 **Coral Types:**

- **Lobe Coral & Finger Coral** – Abundant throughout the bay
- **Cauliflower Coral** – Found in deeper waters

Visitor Services & Amenities

- ✔️ **Snorkel Gear Rental** – Available on-site (**$20 per set**)
- ✔️ **Restrooms & Showers** – Convenient facilities near the entrance

✔ **Snack Bar** – Located near the parking lot (**food/drinks prohibited on the beach**)

Safety Tips & Conservation Rules

▲ **No touching coral** – Damages fragile marine ecosystems
▲ **Apply reef-safe sunscreen** – Chemical sunscreens harm marine life
▲ **Lifeguards on duty** – Always follow their advice
▲ **Strong currents past the reef** – Stay within designated snorkeling areas

Insider Tips

▪ **Arrive before 7 AM** – Best chance of getting parking and calm waters
▪ **Bring water shoes** – Some areas have sharp coral and rocky patches
▪ **Watch the educational video** – Required before entering to learn conservation practices

Shark's Cove (Pūpūkea Marine Life Conservation District)

Historical Background

Despite its name, **Shark's Cove** isn't known for sharks! According to **Hawaiian legend**, the cove's unique **lava rock formations resemble shark teeth**. This area is part of the **Pūpūkea Marine Life Conservation District**, meaning **no fishing is allowed**, ensuring its **marine biodiversity thrives**.

Location & Accessibility

📍 **Address:** Kamehameha Hwy, Haleiwa, HI 96712
🏝 **Location: North Shore Oahu**, between **Waimea Bay & Three Tables Beach**
🚗 **Parking:** Free parking lot across the street

Entrance Fees

💲 **Free Admission** – No reservations required

Opening Hours

⏰ **Open 24/7** – Best snorkeling during daylight hours

Best Time to Visit

☀ **Summer (May – September)** – Calm waters, best visibility
🌊 **Avoid Winter (October – April)** – Huge waves & strong currents make it unsafe

Snorkeling & Diving Experience

Shark's Cove offers **a different snorkeling experience** compared to Hanauma Bay. Instead of sandy beaches, the **shoreline is rocky and volcanic**, creating an **underwater maze of lava tubes, caves, and tide pools**. It's **best suited for intermediate to advanced snorkelers** due to occasional **strong currents**.

🐟 **Common Marine Species:**

- **Hawaiian Green Sea Turtles** – Often spotted near lava ledges
- **Hawaiian Spinner Dolphins** – Occasionally seen offshore
- **Moorish Idol & Butterflyfish** – Strikingly colorful fish species
- **Hawaiian Moray Eels** – Peek out from lava rock crevices
- **White Tip Reef Sharks (Rare but Possible)** – Sometimes seen deeper in caves

🌊 **Diving Spots:**
🐚 **Underwater Lava Tubes & Caves** – Unique swim-through formations for divers
🪨 **Deep Pools (10–25 ft)** – Great visibility for observing larger marine life

Visitor Services & Amenities

✔ **Snorkel Gear Rental Nearby** – Available in Haleiwa Town
✔ **Restrooms & Showers** – Basic facilities across the street
✔ **Food Trucks & Cafes** – Several options within walking distance

Safety Tips & Conservation Rules

⚠ **No lifeguards on duty** – Snorkel with a buddy
⚠ **Winter months are dangerous** – Avoid during high surf season
⚠ **Wear reef shoes** – Rocky shoreline can be slippery and sharp
⚠ **Watch for waves** – Sudden swells can push swimmers into rocks

Insider Tips

▪ **Visit in the morning (8-10 AM)** – Less crowded, best visibility
▪ **Look for tide pools** – Great for exploring smaller marine creatures
▪ **Check surf reports** – If waves are over **3 feet**, snorkeling is not safe

Summary

Hanauma Bay vs. Shark's Cove – Which One to Choose?

Feature	Hanauma Bay	Shark's Cove
Best For	Beginner snorkelers, families	Intermediate/Advanced snorkelers & divers
Marine Life	Turtles, tropical fish, coral reefs	Turtles, dolphins, eels, reef sharks
Water Conditions	Calm, shallow waters	Rocky, deeper waters with caves
Fees	$25 entry + parking fee	Free
Facilities	Rentals, restrooms, lifeguards	Basic restrooms, no lifeguards
Best Season	Year-round	Summer (May – September)

Both sites offer **stunning underwater experiences**, making them **must-visit snorkeling and diving spots in Oahu**.

5.3 Surfing: Best Spots for Beginners and Pros

Oahu is the **birthplace of modern surfing** and home to some of the **most legendary waves in the world**. From **gentle beginner-friendly breaks** in Waikiki to **massive, adrenaline-pumping waves** on the North Shore, Oahu has something for every surfer. Whether you're just starting or looking to ride world-class barrels, here's a **detailed guide to the best surf spots for beginners and pros**.

🌊 Best Surf Spots for Beginners

If you're new to surfing, Oahu offers **calm, consistent waves** and **soft sandy breaks** that make learning safe and enjoyable. Here are the top spots to catch your first waves.

1. Waikiki Beach

- 📍 **Location:** South Shore, Honolulu
- 💲 **Cost:** Free (Board rentals $10–$30 per hour)
- 🌊 **Wave Type:** Long, slow-breaking waves (1–3 ft)
- 🏖️ **Best For:** First-time surfers, families

Description & Experience

Waikiki Beach is **one of the best places in the world to learn to surf**. The long, rolling waves make it easy to stand up and ride for **extended distances**. Several surf schools line the shore, offering **lessons and board rentals**.

Best Surf Schools

- ✔️ **Hans Hedemann Surf School** – Expert instructors, private/group lessons
- ✔️ **Faith Surf School** – Run by a family of pro surfers
- ✔️ **Ty Gurney Surf School** – Personalized coaching for beginners

Tips for Beginners

- ▪ Start with a **longboard (8–10 ft)** – Easier to balance
- ▪ Go **early in the morning** – Fewer crowds, cleaner waves
- ▪ **Watch out for reef areas** – Stick to sandy-bottom spots

2. Ala Moana Beach Park (Magic Island)

- **Location:** South Shore, Honolulu
- **Cost:** Free
- **Wave Type:** Gentle reef break (1–3 ft)
- **Best For:** Beginners looking for uncrowded waves

Description & Experience

Ala Moana Beach Park, just west of Waikiki, offers a **quieter surf experience**. The waves here are **softer** but still provide a good ride for beginners who want to practice without the heavy crowds of Waikiki.

Pros

- ✔ Less crowded than Waikiki
- ✔ Great for practicing turns
- ✔ Easy access from Honolulu hotels

Cons

- ⚠ **Watch for coral reefs** in shallow spots
- ⚠ **Best during mid-to-high tide** to avoid reef exposure

3. White Plains Beach

- **Location:** Ewa Beach (West Oahu)
- **Cost:** Free
- **Wave Type:** Slow-breaking beach break (1–4 ft)
- **Best For:** Beginners who want fewer crowds

Description & Experience

Located on Oahu's **west side**, White Plains Beach offers **gentle, rolling waves** that are perfect for beginners. This area is **less touristy**, giving new surfers **plenty of space** to practice.

Why Beginners Love It

- ✔ **Sandy bottom, fewer reef hazards**
- ✔ **Mellow, consistent waves**
- ✔ **Fewer crowds than Waikiki**

Surfboard Rentals Nearby

🏄 **White Plains Surf Shack** – Affordable board rentals & lessons

🏄 Best Surf Spots for Experienced Surfers

For advanced surfers, Oahu is **home to some of the world's most famous waves**. If you're ready for fast barrels and powerful waves, check out these **top spots**.

1. Banzai Pipeline

- 📍 **Location:** North Shore, Ehukai Beach Park
- 🌊 **Wave Type:** Hollow reef break, barrels (10–30+ ft in winter)
- 🏄 **Best For:** Experts only

Description & Experience

Banzai Pipeline, or just **Pipeline**, is one of the most **dangerous and iconic waves in the world**. Its **perfect, hollow barrels** make it a dream for pro surfers, but its **shallow reef and powerful waves** make it extremely dangerous.

Best Time to Surf

- ✔ **Winter (November – March)** – Biggest swells
- ✔ **Morning sessions** – Glassy conditions

Dangers & Warnings

- ⚠ **Not for beginners** – Heavy waves break over sharp coral
- ⚠ **Strong rip currents** – Only attempt if experienced

2. Waimea Bay

- 📍 **Location:** North Shore
- 🌊 **Wave Type:** Massive, powerful waves (20–40 ft in winter)
- 🏄 **Best For:** Big wave surfers

Description & Experience

Waimea Bay is **legendary** in the world of big-wave surfing. It's known for **some of the largest waves on the planet**, attracting elite surfers every winter. The **Eddie Aikau Big Wave Invitational** is held here when conditions permit.

Best Time to Surf

✔ **Winter (December – February)** – When swells reach 30+ feet
✔ **Low wind conditions** – Best for clean rides

Dangers & Warnings

⚠ **For professionals only** – Strong rip currents, heavy wipeouts
⚠ **Crowded lineups** – Respect local surfers

3. Sunset Beach

📍 **Location:** North Shore
🌊 **Wave Type:** Long, powerful waves (6–25 ft in winter)
🏄 **Best For:** Advanced surfers

Description & Experience

Sunset Beach is a **long, shifting wave** that offers incredible **barrels and steep drops**. It's one of the **most technical waves** on the North Shore, requiring precise timing and skill.

Best Time to Surf

✔ **Winter (November – February)** – Biggest swells
✔ **Offshore wind days** – Creates clean barrels

Dangers & Warnings

⚠ **Strong rip currents** – Paddling out is difficult
⚠ **Sharp reef** – Falls can be dangerous

🏆 Summary: Best Surf Spots Based on Skill Level

Surf Spot	Best For	Wave Size	Wave Type
Waikiki Beach	Beginners	1–3 ft	Long, gentle waves
Ala Moana Beach Park	Beginners	1–3 ft	Soft reef break

White Plains Beach	Beginners	1–4 ft	Beach break
Banzai Pipeline	Experts	10–30+ ft	Hollow, barreling reef break
Waimea Bay	Big Wave Surfers	20–40+ ft	Heavy, steep drop waves
Sunset Beach	Advanced	6–25 ft	Fast, long rides

★ Insider Surfing Tips for Oahu

- **Check surf reports daily** – Use apps like **Surfline** or **MagicSeaweed**
- **Respect local surfers** – Follow lineup etiquette
- **Bring reef-safe sunscreen** – Protect yourself and the ocean
- **Wear surf booties in reef areas** – Helps avoid cuts from coral
- **Watch the waves before paddling out** – Learn the breaks and rip currents

Chapter 6. Where to Stay: Accommodation Options in Oahu

6.1 Luxury Resorts: Four Seasons Resort Oahu, The Ritz-Carlton Residences Waikiki Beach

Oahu is home to **world-class luxury resorts**, offering **top-tier accommodations, breathtaking ocean views, and premium amenities**. Whether you're seeking **secluded beachfront opulence** or a **high-end urban retreat**, Oahu has something to offer. Below are two of the **best luxury resorts on the island**, featuring detailed information on **location, pricing, services, and key features**.

🌺 Four Seasons Resort Oahu at Ko Olina

- 📍 **Address:** 92-1001 Olani St, Kapolei, HI 96707, USA
- 📞 **Contact:** +1 808-679-0079
- 🌐 **Website:** www.fourseasons.com/oahu
- 💲 **Price Range:** $900 – $5,000+ per night (varies by season and room type)
- 📌 **Location:** West Oahu, in the exclusive Ko Olina resort area, approximately **40 minutes from Honolulu International Airport (HNL)**

🏨 Overview & Experience

The **Four Seasons Resort Oahu at Ko Olina** offers **ultra-luxurious beachfront accommodations** in a **secluded paradise**. Overlooking the **pristine lagoons of Ko Olina**, this resort is a top choice for travelers looking for **elegance, relaxation, and exclusivity**. The **white-sand beaches, lush tropical gardens, and world-class amenities** make it a **favorite among celebrities and honeymooners**.

🌟 Key Features & Highlights

✔ Spacious oceanfront suites with private lanais (balconies)
✔ Five-star dining options, including the renowned La Hiki Steakhouse
✔ Adults-only infinity pool & lagoon-style family pool
✔ Naupaka Spa & Wellness Center offering traditional Hawaiian therapies
✔ Championship golf course at Ko Olina Golf Club nearby
✔ Private beach access with snorkeling, paddleboarding, and canoeing

🛎 Visitor Services & Amenities

✔ 24/7 concierge & butler service
✔ Complimentary beach equipment & cabana rentals
✔ Luxury airport transfers & chauffeur services
✔ Babysitting services & kids' club for families
✔ On-site fitness center & yoga classes
✔ Private yacht charters available for island excursions

💡 Who Should Stay Here?

▪ **Honeymooners & Couples** – Romantic setting with sunset views
▪ **Luxury Travelers** – World-class service and five-star amenities
▪ **Families** – Kid-friendly pools, private beaches, and kids' club

🏨 The Ritz-Carlton Residences, Waikiki Beach

📍 **Address:** 383 Kalaimoku St, Honolulu, HI 96815, USA
📞 **Contact:** +1 808-922-8111
🌐 **Website:** www.ritzcarlton.com/en/hotels/hawaii/waikiki
💲 **Price Range:** $800 – $4,500+ per night
📌 **Location:** Heart of **Waikiki**, near **Luxury Row**, just **20 minutes from Honolulu International Airport (HNL)**

🏨 Overview & Experience

Unlike traditional resorts, **The Ritz-Carlton Residences, Waikiki Beach** is a **luxury residential-style hotel** that provides **five-star service** with the **comfort of a private home**. Located in **bustling Waikiki**, this high-rise retreat offers **unparalleled views of the Pacific Ocean**, stylish accommodations, and **convenient access to Honolulu's best dining, shopping, and nightlife**.

🌟 Key Features & Highlights

✔ Spacious residential-style suites with gourmet kitchens
✔ Floor-to-ceiling windows offering panoramic ocean views
✔ Infinity pools with cabanas overlooking Waikiki Beach
✔ World-class spa featuring Hawaiian-inspired treatments
✔ Michelin-star dining at Sushi Sho & La Vie French restaurant
✔ Exclusive shopping access to Waikiki's Luxury Row

🛎 Visitor Services & Amenities

✔ Personal concierge services available 24/7
✔ Valet parking & private transportation services
✔ Pet-friendly accommodations with luxury pet services
✔ State-of-the-art fitness center & yoga studio
✔ Rooftop infinity pools with private cabanas
✔ Private chef services available for in-room dining

💡 Who Should Stay Here?

🔲 **Luxury Shoppers & Business Travelers** – Walking distance to **Luxury Row**
🔲 **Couples & Honeymooners** – Elegant, private, and romantic atmosphere
🔲 **Families & Long-Term Stays** – Spacious suites with full kitchens

🏆 Which Luxury Resort is Right for You?

Resort	Location	Price Range	Best For	Key Features
Four Seasons Resort Oahu	Ko Olina (West Oahu)	$900 – $5,000+	Honeymooners, Luxury Travelers, Families	Beachfront, Infinity Pool, Private Lagoon

| Ritz-Carlton Residences | Waikiki (Honolulu) | $800 – $4,500+ | – | Business Travelers, Luxury Couples, Long Stays | Rooftop Pool, Shopping, Full Kitchens |

📍 **Insider Tips for Booking Luxury Resorts in Oahu**

✔️ **Book early for peak season (December – April)** – Resorts fill up fast during winter
✔️ **Check for resort fees** – Some luxury resorts add **daily resort fees ($40–$60)**
✔️ **Use loyalty programs** – Four Seasons and Ritz-Carlton offer VIP perks for members
✔️ **Look for special packages** – Many resorts offer honeymoon or adventure packages
✔️ **Request ocean-view suites** – The best rooms have **uninterrupted Pacific views**

6.2 Mid-Range Hotels: Hilton Hawaiian Village & Moana Surfrider

Oahu has an array of **mid-range hotels** that offer **comfort, prime locations, and great amenities** without the high-end luxury price tag. These hotels cater to **families, couples, and solo travelers** looking for a **relaxing yet affordable** stay. Below are two of the **best mid-range hotels in Oahu—Hilton Hawaiian Village and Moana Surfrider**—with details on **location, pricing, services, and key features**.

🌴 **Hilton Hawaiian Village Waikiki Beach Resort**

📍 **Address:** 2005 Kalia Rd, Honolulu, HI 96815, USA
📞 **Contact:** +1 808-949-4321
🌐 **Website:** www.hiltonhawaiianvillage.com
💲 **Price Range:** $300 – $700 per night (varies by season and room type)
📌 **Location:** Waikiki Beach, **10 minutes from downtown Honolulu and 20 minutes from Honolulu International Airport (HNL)**

🏨 **Overview & Experience**

The **Hilton Hawaiian Village Waikiki Beach Resort** is one of the **largest and most family-friendly resorts in Oahu**. Set on **22 acres of beachfront property**, the resort features **five hotel towers**, multiple pools, and **an expansive lagoon**. It's an excellent option for those who want **resort-style amenities** at a **mid-range price**.

🌺 Key Features & Highlights

✔️ Five hotel towers with ocean, city, and garden-view rooms
✔️ Duke Kahanamoku Lagoon – a private saltwater lagoon for swimming & paddleboarding
✔️ Six swimming pools, including the Paradise Pool with waterslides
✔️ Nightly entertainment, including a Friday night fireworks show
✔️ 20+ on-site restaurants, including Bali Steak & Seafood and Tropics Bar & Grill
✔️ Direct beach access with water sports rentals available

🛎️ Visitor Services & Amenities

✔️ Concierge services for booking island tours & excursions
✔️ Spa & wellness center offering Hawaiian-inspired treatments
✔️ Family-friendly activities, including hula lessons & lei-making workshops
✔️ Kids' program & babysitting services available
✔️ Fitness center & yoga classes
✔️ Shopping complex with boutiques & gift shops

💡 Who Should Stay Here?

🟫 **Families** – Kid-friendly pools, activities, and a private lagoon
🟫 **Travelers Who Want Convenience** – Everything is on-site, including dining & shops
🟫 **First-Time Visitors** – Central location with easy access to Waikiki attractions

🌴 Moana Surfrider, A Westin Resort & Spa

📍 **Address:** 2365 Kalakaua Ave, Honolulu, HI 96815, USA
📞 **Contact:** +1 808-922-3111
🌐 **Website:** www.moana-surfrider.com
💲 **Price Range:** $350 – $800 per night
📌 **Location:** Waikiki Beach, right on **Kalakaua Avenue**, **20 minutes from Honolulu International Airport (HNL)**

🏨 Overview & Experience

Known as the **"First Lady of Waikiki"**, **Moana Surfrider** is one of Oahu's most **historic** and **charming** hotels. Built in **1901**, this elegant beachfront resort combines **old-world charm** with **modern comfort**. The **stunning colonial-style**

architecture, oceanfront location, and **serene ambiance** make it a **perfect choice for couples and history lovers**.

🌟 Key Features & Highlights

✔ Classic colonial-style hotel with a historic ambiance
✔ Prime beachfront location with direct Waikiki Beach access
✔ Iconic Banyan Tree Courtyard with oceanfront seating
✔ Award-winning Moana Lani Spa with oceanfront treatment rooms
✔ Elegant oceanfront dining at Beachhouse at the Moana
✔ Afternoon tea service in the Veranda, inspired by British traditions

🛎 Visitor Services & Amenities

✔ 24-hour concierge & front desk service
✔ Beachside pool with cabanas available for rent
✔ Fitness center & yoga classes with ocean views
✔ Cultural programs, including lei-making & ukulele lessons
✔ Live Hawaiian music performances in the evenings
✔ Bike rentals available for exploring Waikiki

💡 Who Should Stay Here?

▪ **Couples & Honeymooners** – Romantic beachfront setting with old-world charm
▪ **History & Culture Lovers** – Stay at one of Hawaii's most historic hotels
▪ **Luxury Travelers on a Budget** – Enjoy luxury at a mid-range price

🏆 Which Mid-Range Hotel is Right for You?

Hotel	Location	Price Range	Best For	Key Features
Hilton Hawaiian Village	Waikiki Beach	$300 – $700	Families, First-Time Visitors	Private Lagoon, Waterslides, Multiple Pools
Moana Surfrider	Waikiki Beach	$350 – $800	Couples, History Lovers	Colonial Charm,

Beachfront Tea Service, Spa

💡 Insider Tips for Booking Mid-Range Hotels in Oahu

✔️ **Book in advance** – Prices rise significantly during peak seasons (**December – April** & **June – August**)
✔️ **Check for resort fees** – Many hotels charge a daily fee of **$35 – $50 per night**
✔️ **Request ocean-view rooms** – Not all rooms have direct ocean views, so ask when booking
✔️ **Look for package deals** – Some hotels offer discounts when bundled with flights or car rentals
✔️ **Stay flexible with dates** – Rates tend to be lower on weekdays compared to weekends

6.3 Budget-Friendly Stays in Oahu

Oahu is often associated with **luxury resorts and high-end hotels**, but there are **affordable accommodation options** for travelers on a **budget**. Whether you're a **solo backpacker, student, or traveler looking for a great deal**, you can still experience **Oahu's beautiful beaches, cultural sites, and outdoor adventures** without overspending.

Here are two of the **best budget-friendly stays in Oahu—The Surfjack Hotel & Swim Club** and **Polynesian Hostel Beach Club**—with details on **location, pricing, amenities, and key features**.

🛎 The Surfjack Hotel & Swim Club

📍 **Address:** 412 Lewers St, Honolulu, HI 96815, USA
📞 **Contact:** +1 808-923-8882
🌐 **Website:** www.surfjack.com
💲 **Price Range:** $150 – $300 per night

📍 **Location: Waikiki**, within walking distance of Waikiki Beach, restaurants, and shopping

🏨 **Overview & Experience**

The **Surfjack Hotel & Swim Club** is a stylish, retro-inspired boutique hotel that offers an **affordable yet trendy stay** in **Waikiki**. This hotel is perfect for **young travelers, couples, and digital nomads** who want a **laid-back atmosphere** without the high price tag. The **vintage Hawaiian decor, lively social scene, and unique poolside events** make it a fun alternative to larger resorts.

🌟 **Key Features & Highlights**

✔️ Trendy, retro-style boutique hotel with a creative atmosphere
✔️ Instagram-worthy pool with "Wish You Were Here" painted at the bottom
✔️ On-site restaurant, Mahina & Sun's, featuring farm-to-table Hawaiian cuisine
✔️ Live music, film screenings, and creative workshops for guests
✔️ Bikes available for rent to explore Waikiki
✔️ Walking distance to Waikiki Beach, shops, and bars

🛎️ **Visitor Services & Amenities**

✔️ Concierge service for booking activities & tours
✔️ Outdoor swimming pool with sun loungers
✔️ Complimentary morning coffee & tea for guests
✔️ Pet-friendly rooms available
✔️ Free WiFi & work-friendly spaces for remote workers

💡 **Who Should Stay Here?**

🏨 **Young travelers & couples** – Stylish, social, and budget-friendly
🏨 **Solo adventurers & digital nomads** – Great communal spaces & work-friendly environment
🏨 **Travelers who want a unique boutique experience** – A hip alternative to traditional hotels

🏨 **Polynesian Hostel Beach Club**

📍 **Address:** 2584 Lemon Rd, Honolulu, HI 96815, USA
📞 **Contact:** +1 808-922-1340
🌐 **Website:** www.polynesianhostel.com
💲 **Price Range:** $50 – $120 per night (Dorms & Private Rooms Available)

📍 **Location: 1 block from Waikiki Beach**, next to the Honolulu Zoo & Kapiolani Park

🏨 **Overview & Experience**

For budget travelers looking for **a social atmosphere and prime location**, the **Polynesian Hostel Beach Club** is one of the **best hostels in Oahu**. It offers **affordable dorm-style accommodations and private rooms**, making it a top choice for **backpackers, solo travelers, and students**. The hostel is located **just steps from Waikiki Beach**, providing **easy access to surfing, hiking, and nightlife**.

🌟 **Key Features & Highlights**

✔️ Affordable dorm-style & private rooms
✔️ 1-minute walk to Waikiki Beach, great for surfers & beach lovers
✔️ Free daily breakfast & coffee for guests
✔️ Outdoor communal area with BBQ and social events
✔️ Fully equipped communal kitchen for budget-conscious travelers
✔️ Bike & surfboard rentals available on-site

🛎️ **Visitor Services & Amenities**

✔️ Tour booking assistance for island activities
✔️ Free WiFi throughout the hostel
✔️ Lockers available for valuables
✔️ Laundry facilities on-site
✔️ Budget-friendly airport shuttle service available

💡 **Who Should Stay Here?**

▪️ **Backpackers & solo travelers** – Social atmosphere, great for meeting people
▪️ **Surfers & beach lovers** – Steps away from Waikiki Beach & surf spots
▪️ **Students & young travelers** – Affordable accommodations with a fun vibe

🏆 **Which Budget Stay is Right for You?**

Hotel/Hostel	Location	Price Range	Best For	Key Features
Surfjack Hotel & Swim Club	Waikiki	$150 – $300	Young Travelers, Digital Nomads	Trendy Decor, Pool, Events
Polynesian Hostel Beach Club	Waikiki	$50 – $120	Backpackers, Solo Travelers	Steps to Beach, Free Breakfast, Social Atmosphere

💡 **Insider Tips for Booking Budget Stays in Oahu**

✔️ **Book early** – Budget-friendly stays fill up fast, especially during peak travel months
✔️ **Consider hostels for savings** – If you don't mind dorms, you can save big on accommodations
✔️ **Check for hidden fees** – Some places charge extra for towels, WiFi, or resort fees
✔️ **Look for package deals** – Some hotels offer discounts for longer stays or booking tours with them
✔️ **Use public transportation** – If you're staying in Waikiki, you may not need a rental car

🔎 **Summary**

If you're traveling to Oahu on a **budget**, you don't have to sacrifice **comfort or location**. The **Surfjack Hotel & Swim Club** is a **stylish, mid-range option** for those who want a **boutique feel with fun social events**, while the **Polynesian Hostel Beach Club** is perfect for **backpackers and budget travelers** looking for a **cheap stay near Waikiki Beach**.

6.4 Vacation Rentals and Boutique Stays in Oahu

For travelers seeking a **home-away-from-home experience**, Oahu offers a variety of **vacation rentals and boutique stays**. Whether you're looking for a **secluded beachfront villa, a stylish boutique hotel, or a cozy rental apartment**, there are plenty of options to suit different budgets and preferences.

This section highlights some of the **best vacation rentals and boutique stays in Oahu**, complete with **location details, pricing, key features, and visitor services** to help you choose the perfect accommodation.

🏝 Vacation Rentals in Oahu

Vacation rentals provide the **flexibility of a private home**, making them ideal for **families, groups, and travelers who prefer a more independent stay**. Popular options include **beachfront condos, jungle retreats, and city apartments** in Waikiki.

1️⃣ North Shore Beachfront Villa

- 📍 **Location:** Haleiwa, North Shore, Oahu
- 💲 **Price Range:** $400 – $800 per night
- 🌐 **Website:** Available on **Airbnb & VRBO**

🌟 Key Features & Highlights

- ✔ Steps from the beach with direct ocean access
- ✔ Fully equipped kitchen & outdoor BBQ area
- ✔ Private lanai (balcony) with stunning sunset views
- ✔ Spacious living area, ideal for families or groups
- ✔ Close to famous surf spots like Banzai Pipeline

🛎 Visitor Services & Amenities

- ✔ Free WiFi & Smart TV
- ✔ Beach gear (chairs, umbrellas, snorkeling equipment)
- ✔ Self-check-in for added convenience
- ✔ Parking space included

💡 **Best for:** Families, surfers, and travelers looking for a **quiet, beachfront retreat** away from Waikiki crowds.

2 Waikiki Luxury Condo with Ocean Views

- **Location:** Waikiki, Honolulu
- **Price Range:** $200 – $500 per night
- **Website:** Available on **Airbnb & VRBO**

Key Features & Highlights

- ✔ Panoramic views of Waikiki Beach & Diamond Head
- ✔ Access to a rooftop pool & fitness center
- ✔ Walking distance to restaurants, shopping, and nightlife
- ✔ Fully equipped kitchen & modern decor

Visitor Services & Amenities

- ✔ High-speed WiFi & workspace for remote workers
- ✔ Washer & dryer in unit
- ✔ Private parking available

Best for: Couples and travelers who want **a luxury experience in the heart of Waikiki** without staying in a hotel.

Boutique Stays in Oahu

Boutique hotels in Oahu offer **charming, intimate accommodations** with personalized service and stylish decor. These hotels are **smaller than traditional resorts**, making them perfect for travelers who **prefer a unique and less crowded stay**.

3 The Laylow, Autograph Collection

- **Location:** 2299 Kuhio Ave, Honolulu, HI 96815
- **Contact:** +1 808-922-6600
- **Website:** www.thelaylow.com
- **Price Range:** $250 – $450 per night

Key Features & Highlights

- ✔ Trendy mid-century modern decor with Hawaiian vibes
- ✔ Lush outdoor seating areas & rooftop bar
- ✔ Central Waikiki location, minutes from the beach
- ✔ Live music, social events, and local art displays

🛎️ **Visitor Services & Amenities**

✔️ Complimentary welcome basket with Hawaiian snacks
✔️ 24-hour fitness center & pool
✔️ Pet-friendly accommodations

📍 **Best for:** Couples, solo travelers, and those looking for a **hip, stylish boutique stay** in Waikiki.

4️⃣ Lotus Honolulu at Diamond Head

📍 **Location:** 2885 Kalakaua Ave, Honolulu, HI 96815
📞 **Contact:** +1 808-922-1700
🌐 **Website:** www.lotushonoluluhotel.com
💲 **Price Range:** $300 – $600 per night

🌺 **Key Features & Highlights**

✔️ Quiet, peaceful retreat near Diamond Head
✔️ Lush garden surroundings & ocean views
✔️ Complimentary bike rentals & yoga classes
✔️ Short walk to Kapiolani Park & Waikiki Beach

🛎️ **Visitor Services & Amenities**

✔️ Free morning coffee & tea service
✔️ On-site restaurant with locally sourced ingredients
✔️ Spacious balconies in every room

📍 **Best for:** Travelers seeking a **tranquil, nature-inspired stay** away from Waikiki's busy crowds.

🏆 **Which Option is Right for You?**

Accommodation	Location	Price Range	Best For	Key Features
North Shore Beachfront Villa	North Shore	$400 – $800	Families, surfers, quiet retreat	Private beach access, full

				kitchen, sunset views
Waikiki Luxury Condo	Waikiki	$200 – $500	Couples, city lovers, remote workers	Rooftop pool, modern design, ocean views
The Laylow, Autograph Collection	Waikiki	$250 – $450	Solo travelers, trendy travelers	Hip decor, rooftop bar, central location
Lotus Honolulu at Diamond Head	Near Diamond Head	$300 – $600	Nature lovers, peaceful retreat	Garden setting, yoga classes, ocean views

💡 Insider Tips for Booking Vacation Rentals & Boutique Stays

✔️ **Book in advance:** Oahu's best rentals and boutique stays fill up quickly, especially during peak season.
✔️ **Check for hidden fees:** Some vacation rentals charge cleaning fees, service fees, and security deposits.
✔️ **Read reviews:** Look for recent reviews to ensure the accommodation meets your expectations.
✔️ **Consider location:** Choose based on your activities—Waikiki for city life, North Shore for beaches, and Diamond Head for a quiet retreat.
✔️ **Look for added perks:** Some rentals offer **free parking, beach gear, or discount codes for local tours**.

🔎 Summary

If you're looking for a **personalized, stylish, and unique stay** in Oahu, **vacation rentals and boutique hotels** offer fantastic alternatives to traditional resorts.

🏡 **Vacation Rentals:** Best for **families, groups, and travelers wanting extra space and privacy**. Options like the **North Shore Beachfront Villa** and **Waikiki Luxury Condo** offer **prime locations with home-like amenities**.

🏨 **Boutique Hotels:** Perfect for **couples and solo travelers seeking a more intimate, stylish experience**. The **Laylow** is ideal for trendy travelers, while **Lotus Honolulu** offers a **peaceful retreat near Diamond Head**.

Chapter 7. Oahu's Food and Dining Scene

7.1 Best Local Hawaiian Dishes to Try

Hawaiian cuisine is a unique blend of **Native Hawaiian, Polynesian, Asian, and American influences**, resulting in a delicious and diverse food culture. Whether you're craving fresh seafood, slow-roasted meats, or tropical desserts, Oahu offers an incredible culinary experience.

Here's a detailed **guide to the must-try local Hawaiian dishes**, including their history, key ingredients, and where to find the best versions on the island.

🍡 1. Poke (Hawaiian-Style Sashimi)

🌿 About the Dish

Poke (pronounced "poh-kay") is a traditional **Hawaiian raw fish salad**, typically made with **ahi (yellowfin tuna)**, soy sauce, sesame oil, seaweed, and onions. This dish has deep roots in Hawaiian culture, dating back to ancient Polynesian settlers who seasoned freshly caught fish with sea salt and kukui nut.

🍽 Where to Try It

📍 **Ono Seafood** – 747 Kapahulu Ave, Honolulu, HI
💲 **Price:** $12 – $18 per bowl
🌐 **Website:** www.onoseafood.com
🔥 **Why Go?** Known for some of the freshest poke on the island, made daily with premium fish.

📍 **Tamura's Fine Wine & Liquors** – Multiple locations in Oahu
💲 **Price:** $10 – $16 per pound
🌐 **Website:** www.tamurasfinewine.com
🔥 **Why Go?** A hidden gem for **locals** looking for high-quality, freshly prepared poke.

🍡 2. Kalua Pig (Smoked Hawaiian-Style Pork)

🌿 About the Dish

Kalua Pig is a **slow-roasted, shredded pork dish** traditionally cooked in an **imu (underground oven)**. The smoky, tender pork is flavored only with **Hawaiian sea salt and natural juices**, making it one of the most authentic Hawaiian dishes.

🍽 Where to Try It

📍 **Helena's Hawaiian Food** – 1240 N School St, Honolulu, HI
💲 **Price:** $15 – $25 per plate
🌐 **Website:** www.helenashawaiianfood.com
🔥 **Why Go?** A James Beard Award-winning restaurant serving traditional Hawaiian dishes since 1946.

📍 **Highway Inn** – 680 Ala Moana Blvd, Honolulu, HI
💲 **Price:** $14 – $22 per plate
🌐 **Website:** www.myhighwayinn.com
🔥 **Why Go?** A **local favorite** for authentic Hawaiian plate lunches, including **kalua pork, poi, and laulau**.

3. Haupia (Coconut Pudding)

About the Dish

Haupia is a **creamy coconut pudding** made from **coconut milk, sugar, and cornstarch**. It's often served as a **dessert** or a topping for pies and cakes. This traditional treat has been a staple in Hawaiian cuisine for centuries.

Where to Try It

Ted's Bakery – 59-024 Kamehameha Hwy, Haleiwa, HI
Price: $4 – $7 per slice (Haupia Pie)
Website: www.tedsbakery.com
Why Go? Famous for their **Chocolate Haupia Cream Pie**, a delicious mix of rich chocolate and creamy coconut pudding.

Liliha Bakery – 580 N Nimitz Hwy, Honolulu, HI
Price: $3 – $6 per serving
Website: www.lilihabakery.com
Why Go? A legendary Hawaiian bakery serving **traditional pastries and desserts**, including **haupia cakes and puffs**.

4. Loco Moco (Hawaiian Comfort Food)

About the Dish

Loco Moco is a **hearty, local comfort dish** made with **white rice, a hamburger patty, brown gravy, and a fried egg on top**. It's believed to have originated in **Hilo, Hawaii, in the 1940s**, when local surfers and students wanted a cheap and filling meal.

Where to Try It

Rainbow Drive-In – 3308 Kanaina Ave, Honolulu, HI
Price: $10 – $15 per plate
Website: www.rainbowdrivein.com
Why Go? An iconic spot serving **affordable, no-frills Hawaiian plate lunches**.

📍 **Eggs 'n Things** – Multiple locations in Oahu
💲 **Price:** $12 – $18 per plate
🌐 **Website:** www.eggsnthings.com
🔥 **Why Go?** A **popular breakfast spot** that offers a **deluxe loco moco** with a variety of gravy and meat options.

🌺 5. Laulau (Steamed Meat Wrapped in Taro Leaves)

🌿 About the Dish

Laulau is a **Hawaiian dish made by wrapping pork, fish, or chicken in taro leaves and steaming it.** The dish was traditionally cooked in an **imu (underground oven)**, allowing the flavors to develop slowly.

🍽 Where to Try It

📍 **Alicia's Market** – 267 Mokauea St, Honolulu, HI
💲 **Price:** $12 – $20 per plate
🌐 **Website:** www.aliciasmarket.com
🔥 **Why Go?** One of the **best takeout spots** for laulau, poke, and Hawaiian plate lunches.

📍 **Young's Fish Market** – 1286 Kalani St, Honolulu, HI
💲 **Price:** $14 – $22 per plate
🌐 **Website:** www.youngsfishmarket.com
🔥 **Why Go?** Family-run since 1951, serving **some of the best laulau and kalua pig** on the island.

🥭 Bonus: Tropical Hawaiian Fruits to Try

🍍 **Pineapple** – Best enjoyed fresh from **Dole Plantation**.
🥭 **Lilikoi (Passion Fruit)** – Used in juices, syrups, and desserts.
🥥 **Coconut** – Enjoy fresh coconut water or **toasted coconut snacks**.
🍌 **Apple Banana** – A smaller, sweeter variety of banana native to Hawaii.

🔎 Summary

Hawaiian cuisine offers **a mix of fresh seafood, slow-cooked meats, and tropical flavors**. Whether you're trying **poke, kalua pig, or a loco moco**, Oahu has no shortage of delicious options.

Dish	Best Place to Try It	Price Range	Why It's a Must-Try
Poke	Ono Seafood, Tamura's	$10 – $18	Fresh Hawaiian-style sashimi
Kalua Pig	Helena's Hawaiian Food	$14 – $25	Smoky, tender, traditional Hawaiian dish
Haupia	Ted's Bakery, Liliha Bakery	$3 – $7	Creamy coconut pudding
Loco Moco	Rainbow Drive-In	$10 – $18	Hearty Hawaiian comfort food
Laulau	Young's Fish Market	$12 – $22	Classic Hawaiian steamed meat dish

7.2 Top Restaurants in Honolulu

Honolulu is home to a diverse and vibrant food scene, offering everything from **authentic Hawaiian cuisine** to **high-end dining experiences** and **casual local favorites**. Whether you're in the mood for fresh seafood, innovative fusion dishes, or classic Hawaiian comfort food, there's a perfect restaurant for every craving.

Here's a detailed guide to the **best restaurants in Honolulu**, including price ranges, addresses, key features, and what makes each one special.

🍀 1. Helena's Hawaiian Food *(Best for Authentic Hawaiian Cuisine)*

📍 **Address:** 1240 N School St, Honolulu, HI 96817
📞 **Contact:** +1 (808) 845-8044
💲 **Price Range:** $15 – $30 per person
🌐 **Website:** www.helenashawaiianfood.com

⭐ Key Features:

✔ James Beard Award-winning Hawaiian restaurant
✔ Specializes in **kalua pig, laulau, poi, and pipikaula short ribs**
✔ Family-owned since 1946

🔥 Why Go?

Helena's is **one of the best places** to experience **authentic Hawaiian flavors**, served in a **casual, no-frills setting**. The **pipikaula short ribs** are a must-try!

🍥 2. Senia *(Best for Upscale Hawaiian-Fusion Cuisine)*

📍 **Address:** 75 N King St, Honolulu, HI 96817
📞 **Contact:** +1 (808) 200-5412
💲 **Price Range:** $75 – $150 per person
🌐 **Website:** www.restaurantsenia.com

⭐ Key Features:

✔ Chef-driven menu with **local Hawaiian ingredients and modern techniques**
✔ Offers **a la carte dining and a multi-course tasting menu**
✔ Elegant, contemporary setting

🔥 **Why Go?**

Senia is **one of the top fine dining experiences** in Honolulu, perfect for a **special occasion** or a night of indulgence.

🐟 3. Alan Wong's Honolulu *(Best for Fine Dining with Hawaiian Ingredients)*

📍 **Address:** 1857 S King St, Honolulu, HI 96826
📞 **Contact:** +1 (808) 949-2526
💲 **Price Range:** $80 – $150 per person
🌐 **Website:** www.alanwongs.com

⭐ **Key Features:**

✔️ Chef Alan Wong is a pioneer of **Hawaii Regional Cuisine**
✔️ Signature dishes include **Ginger Crusted Onaga (red snapper) and Kalua Pig Quesadilla**
✔️ Elegant, award-winning restaurant

🔥 **Why Go?**

Alan Wong's is an **iconic fine-dining destination**, where **local flavors meet high-end culinary techniques**.

🏄 4. Duke's Waikiki *(Best for Beachfront Dining & Fresh Seafood)*

📍 **Address:** 2335 Kalakaua Ave #116, Honolulu, HI 96815
📞 **Contact:** +1 (808) 922-2268
💲 **Price Range:** $25 – $60 per person
🌐 **Website:** www.dukeswaikiki.com

⭐ **Key Features:**

✔️ **Oceanfront dining** with spectacular Waikiki Beach views
✔️ Famous for **fresh fish, prime rib, and their legendary Hula Pie**
✔️ Lively atmosphere with live Hawaiian music

🔥 **Why Go?**

Duke's Waikiki is a **classic Hawaiian dining experience**, named after **surfing legend Duke Kahanamoku**. Perfect for a **romantic sunset dinner** or a casual lunch with a view.

🍖 5. Hy's Steak House *(Best for Premium Steaks & Elegant Ambiance)*

📍 **Address:** 2440 Kuhio Ave, Honolulu, HI 96815
📞 **Contact:** +1 (808) 922-5555
💲 **Price Range:** $80 – $150 per person
🌐 **Website:** www.hyswaikiki.com

⭐ **Key Features:**

✔ **Prime-grade, dry-aged steaks** cooked over **Hawaiian kiawe wood**
✔ Classic, old-school **fine dining atmosphere**
✔ Extensive **wine selection**

🔥 **Why Go?**

Hy's Steak House is one of the **best steakhouses in Hawaii**, perfect for a **luxurious, romantic dinner**.

🍜 6. The Pig & The Lady *(Best for Modern Vietnamese & Asian Fusion)*

📍 **Address:** 83 N King St, Honolulu, HI 96817
📞 **Contact:** +1 (808) 585-8255
💲 **Price Range:** $20 – $50 per person
🌐 **Website:** www.thepigandthelady.com

⭐ **Key Features:**

✔ Famous for **pho, banh mi, and creative fusion dishes**
✔ Inspired by **Vietnamese flavors with a Hawaiian twist**
✔ Casual yet trendy atmosphere

🔥 **Why Go?**

This **highly-rated restaurant** is a local favorite for its **bold flavors, fun ambiance, and innovative dishes**.

🍢 7. Mud Hen Water *(Best for Creative Hawaiian Cuisine)*

📍 **Address:** 3452 Waialae Ave, Honolulu, HI 96816
📞 **Contact:** +1 (808) 737-6000
💲 **Price Range:** $30 – $60 per person
🌐 **Website:** www.mudhenwater.com

⭐ **Key Features:**

✔ Locally-sourced **Hawaiian comfort food with a modern twist**
✔ Signature dishes include **Kim Chee Fried Rice and Grilled He'e (octopus)**
✔ Warm and rustic atmosphere

🔥 **Why Go?**

If you're looking for **a unique take on Hawaiian flavors**, this **James Beard-nominated restaurant** is a must-visit.

🍽 **8. Nico's Pier 38** *(Best for Fresh Seafood & Poke)*

📍 **Address:** 1129 N Nimitz Hwy, Honolulu, HI 96817
📞 **Contact:** +1 (808) 540-1377
💲 **Price Range:** $15 – $35 per person
🌐 **Website:** www.nicospier38.com

⭐ **Key Features:**

✔ Fresh seafood sourced directly from **Honolulu Fish Auction**
✔ Signature dishes include **Ahi Tuna Steak and Furikake Seared Ahi**
✔ Relaxed, harbor-side setting

🔥 **Why Go?**

Nico's is the **best place to try freshly caught fish**, served in a **casual, affordable setting**.

🔍 **Summary: Best Restaurants in Honolulu**

Restaurant	Best For	Price Range	Key Feature
Helena's Hawaiian Food	Authentic Hawaiian cuisine	$15 – $30	Famous for **pipikaula short ribs**
Senia	Upscale Hawaiian fusion	$75 – $150	Chef-driven tasting menus

Restaurant	Cuisine	Price	Notable
Alan Wong's	Fine dining	$80 – $150	**Hawaii Regional Cuisine pioneer**
Duke's Waikiki	Beachfront seafood	$25 – $60	**Hula Pie & live music**
Hy's Steak House	High-end steakhouse	$80 – $150	**Kiawe-wood grilled steaks**
The Pig & The Lady	Vietnamese fusion	$20 – $50	**Creative pho & banh mi**
Mud Hen Water	Modern Hawaiian	$30 – $60	Locally-sourced ingredients
Nico's Pier 38	Fresh seafood	$15 – $35	**Fish straight from the auction**

7.3 Budget-Friendly Eats: Food Trucks and Local Markets

If you want to experience **authentic Hawaiian flavors** without breaking the bank, Honolulu's **food trucks and local markets** offer some of the best meals on the island. From fresh poke bowls to savory garlic shrimp, these budget-friendly spots provide **delicious, high-quality food** at affordable prices.

Here's a detailed guide to the **best budget-friendly eats in Oahu**, including **food trucks, local markets, and must-try dishes**.

🚚 Best Food Trucks in Oahu

1. Giovanni's Shrimp Truck (North Shore) – 🦐 Famous Garlic Shrimp

📍 **Location:** 56-505 Kamehameha Hwy, Kahuku, HI 96731
📞 **Contact:** +1 (808) 293-1839
💲 **Price Range:** $14 – $18 per plate
🌐 **Website:** www.giovannisshrimptruck.com

⭐ **Key Features:**
✔️ **World-famous** garlic shrimp plate
✔️ Cash-only, fast service
✔️ Outdoor picnic-style seating

🔥 **Why Go?**
Giovanni's is a **must-visit** for **shrimp lovers**! Their buttery, garlicky shrimp served with rice is legendary.

2. Mike's Huli Chicken (Kaneohe) – 🍗 Huli Huli Chicken

📍 **Location:** 47-525 Kamehameha Hwy, Kaneohe, HI 96744
📞 **Contact:** +1 (808) 312-1376
💲 **Price Range:** $12 – $16 per plate
🌐 **Website:** www.mikeshulichicken.com

⭐ **Key Features:**
✔️ Chicken **slow-roasted over kiawe wood**, giving it a smoky flavor
✔️ Served with rice, pineapple slaw, and mac salad
✔️ Featured on **Diners, Drive-Ins, and Dives**

🔥 **Why Go?**
Mike's Huli Chicken is **Hawaiian BBQ at its best**, offering juicy, flavorful grilled chicken at a great price.

3. Ono Seafood (Honolulu) – 🐟 Best Poke Bowls

📍 **Location:** 747 Kapahulu Ave, Honolulu, HI 96816
📞 **Contact:** +1 (808) 732-4806
💲 **Price Range:** $12 – $18 per bowl
🌐 **Website:** www.onoseafood.com

⭐ **Key Features:**
✔️ **Fresh, locally-sourced** ahi and salmon poke
✔️ Multiple flavor options: spicy, shoyu, wasabi, and Hawaiian style
✔️ Takeout only, but fast service

🔥 **Why Go?**
If you want **the best, freshest poke in Honolulu**, Ono Seafood is **a local favorite** for its generous portions and high-quality fish.

4. North Shore Tacos (Haleiwa) – 🌮 Hawaiian Tacos

📍 **Location:** 66-250 Kamehameha Hwy, Haleiwa, HI 96712
📞 **Contact:** +1 (808) 637-3443
💲 **Price Range:** $10 – $15 per meal
🌐 **Website:** www.northshoretacos.com

⭐ **Key Features:**
✔️ **Mahi-mahi, shrimp, and Kalua pork tacos**
✔️ House-made **pineapple salsa**
✔️ Laid-back, casual vibe

🔥 **Why Go?**
North Shore Tacos is **a hidden gem** serving some of the **best seafood tacos on the island**, paired with fresh island flavors.

5. Steak Shack (Waikiki) – 🥩 Cheap & Delicious Steak Plates

📍 **Location:** 2161 Kalia Rd, Honolulu, HI 96815
📞 **Contact:** +1 (808) 861-9966
💲 **Price Range:** $10 – $15 per plate

⭐ **Key Features:**
✔️ **Juicy grilled steak over rice and salad**
✔️ **Beachfront location** (great sunset views!)
✔️ **One of the cheapest steak plates in Honolulu**

🔥 **Why Go?**
Steak Shack is a **fantastic budget-friendly spot** where you can enjoy **a satisfying meal right by the beach**.

🗾 Best Local Markets in Oahu

6. KCC Farmers' Market – 🌿 Best for Fresh Local Produce & Snacks

📍 **Location:** 4303 Diamond Head Rd, Honolulu, HI 96816
🕐 **Hours:** Saturdays, 7:30 AM – 11 AM
💲 **Price Range:** $5 – $15 per item
🌐 **Website:** www.hfbf.org/farmers-markets/kcc

⭐ **Key Features:**
✔️ **Farm-fresh fruits, Hawaiian honey, macadamia nuts**
✔️ Local vendors selling **poke, malasadas, and fresh juices**
✔️ Stunning views of Diamond Head

🔥 **Why Go?**
A **must-visit market** for trying **fresh tropical fruits, Hawaiian snacks, and artisanal food** in a lively outdoor setting.

7. Waikiki's International Market Place – 🍍 Great for Quick Bites

📍 **Location:** 2330 Kalakaua Ave, Honolulu, HI 96815
🕐 **Hours:** 11 AM – 10 PM daily
🌐 **Website:** www.shopinternationalmarketplace.com

⭐ **Key Features:**
✔️ Open-air market with **food stalls and street vendors**
✔️ Affordable options like **poke bowls, ramen, and plate lunches**
✔️ Located in **the heart of Waikiki**

🔥 **Why Go?**
If you're looking for **a mix of casual eats and shopping**, this is **a great budget-friendly stop** in Waikiki.

📋 Summary: Best Budget-Friendly Eats in Oahu

Name	Best For	Price Range	Key Feature
Giovanni's Shrimp Truck	Garlic shrimp plates	$14 – $18	Iconic shrimp truck

Mike's Huli Chicken	Hawaiian BBQ	$12 – $16	**Slow-roasted chicken**
Ono Seafood	Poke bowls	$12 – $18	**Fresh, local fish**
North Shore Tacos	Seafood tacos	$10 – $15	**Tropical flavors**
Steak Shack	Steak & rice plates	$10 – $15	**Cheap Waikiki steak**
KCC Farmers' Market	Fresh snacks & produce	$5 – $15	**Hawaiian fruits & honey**
International Market Place	Quick local eats	$10 – $20	**Food stalls & casual dining**

🌴 **Final Tips for Budget-Friendly Dining in Oahu**

■ **Go to food trucks** – They often serve **big portions for a great price**.

■ **Try plate lunches** – Local favorites like **L&L Hawaiian Barbecue** offer affordable meals.

■ **Shop at farmers' markets** – They sell **fresh fruits, local snacks, and cheap street food**.

■ **Eat poke bowls** – They're a **filling, affordable, and healthy option**.

7.4 Traditional Hawaiian Luaus and Cultural Dining Experiences

One of the **best ways to experience Hawaiian culture** is by attending a **traditional luau**. These feasts celebrate the **history, music, dance, and cuisine** of the islands, providing an immersive experience filled with **fire dancing, hula performances, and authentic Hawaiian dishes** like **kalua pig, poi, poke, and haupia**.

Here's a **detailed guide** to the best luaus in Oahu, including **prices, locations, key features, and booking information**.

🌺 **Best Luaus in Oahu**

1. Paradise Cove Luau – 🌅 Sunset Beachfront Luau

📍 **Location:** 92-1089 Ali'inui Dr, Kapolei, HI 96707 (Ko Olina)
📞 **Contact:** +1 (808) 842-5911
💲 **Price Range:** $140 – $230 per person
🌐 **Website:** www.paradisecove.com

⭐ **Key Features:**
✔️ **Stunning oceanfront location** in Ko Olina
✔️ **Traditional Hawaiian games and crafts** before the show
✔️ **Lavish buffet with kalua pig, lomi-lomi salmon, poke, and haupia**
✔️ **Spectacular fire knife dancing and hula performances**

🔥 **Why Go?**
Paradise Cove offers **one of the most immersive and authentic luaus in Oahu**, complete with a **beautiful sunset backdrop** and **interactive cultural activities** before dinner.

2. Germaine's Luau – 🌺 Laid-Back, Family-Friendly Experience

📍 **Location:** 91-119 Olai St, Kapolei, HI 96707
📞 **Contact:** +1 (808) 947-3333
💲 **Price Range:** $135 – $195 per person
🌐 **Website:** www.germainesluau.com

⭐ **Key Features:**
✔️ **Casual, backyard-style atmosphere** on a private beach
✔️ **Fire dancing, hula, and Samoan slap dancing**

✔ **All-you-can-eat buffet** with Hawaiian and Polynesian dishes
✔ **Affordable and great for families**

🔥 **Why Go?**
Germaine's Luau feels **less commercialized** than some other luaus, offering a **more relaxed, intimate experience** with a great blend of **entertainment and delicious food.**

3. Chief's Luau – 🔥 Most Entertaining & Engaging Luau

📍 **Location:** Wet'n'Wild Hawaii, 400 Farrington Hwy, Kapolei, HI 96707
📞 **Contact:** +1 (808) 664-0448
💲 **Price Range:** $160 – $230 per person
🌐 **Website:** www.chiefsluau.com

⭐ **Key Features:**
✔ **Hosted by Chief Sielu**, a world-famous fire knife dancer and comedian
✔ **Highly entertaining and humorous performances**
✔ **Interactive cultural activities** like coconut husking and fire-making
✔ **Delicious buffet** featuring Hawaiian staples

🔥 **Why Go?**
Chief's Luau is **perfect for those who love high-energy entertainment**. The show is **fun, engaging, and filled with humor**, making it a great choice for both couples and families.

4. Toa Luau – 🌿 Small, Authentic Luau in the North Shore

📍 **Location:** Waimea Valley, 59-864 Kamehameha Hwy, Haleiwa, HI 96712
📞 **Contact:** +1 (808) 636-2476
💲 **Price Range:** $135 – $185 per person (includes Waimea Valley admission)
🌐 **Website:** www.toaluau.com

⭐ **Key Features:**
✔ **Intimate, small-group setting** (less commercialized)
✔ **Hands-on cultural activities** like taro pounding and coconut tree climbing
✔ **Located in beautiful Waimea Valley** (includes access to the waterfall)
✔ **Locally sourced food with Hawaiian and Samoan dishes**

🔥 **Why Go?**
Toa Luau is **a hidden gem for those wanting a more authentic and cultural**

experience. It's **less touristy and more immersive**, with **hands-on activities** before the show.

5. Ka Moana Luau – 🌙 Best Luau with an Oceanfront View

📍 **Location:** Aloha Tower, 1 Aloha Tower Dr, Honolulu, HI 96813
📞 **Contact:** +1 (808) 926-3800
💲 **Price Range:** $135 – $195 per person
🌐 **Website:** www.moanaluau.com

⭐ **Key Features:**
✔️ **Gorgeous oceanfront setting** at Aloha Tower
✔️ **Polynesian storytelling and dance performances**
✔️ **Interactive activities** like lei-making and coconut husking
✔️ **Farm-to-table buffet** with locally sourced ingredients

🔥 **Why Go?**
Ka Moana Luau is **a fantastic choice for those staying in Honolulu** who want **an oceanfront luau experience without leaving the city**.

🌑 **What to Expect at a Traditional Hawaiian Luau**

A Hawaiian luau is more than just dinner—it's a **celebration of Hawaiian history, traditions, and hospitality**. Here's what you can typically expect:

🟫 **Lei Greeting** – Guests receive a traditional **flower or shell lei** upon arrival.
🟫 **Hawaiian Cultural Activities** – Some luaus offer **coconut husking, hula lessons, ukulele playing, and crafts**.
🟫 **The Imu Ceremony** – Witness the traditional **unearthing of the kalua pig**, cooked underground in an **imu (Hawaiian oven)**.
🟫 **Buffet Feast** – Luaus usually serve a variety of traditional dishes like:

- **Kalua Pig** – Slow-cooked, smoky pork
- **Poi** – Taro root paste (a Hawaiian staple)
- **Lomi-Lomi Salmon** – Fresh, marinated salmon salad
- **Poke** – Cubed, marinated raw fish
- **Haupia** – Coconut pudding for dessert
  🟫 **Live Entertainment** – Enjoy **hula dancing, fire knife performances, Tahitian drumming, and storytelling**.

📋 Summary: Best Luaus in Oahu

Luau	Best For	Price Range	Location	Key Features
Paradise Cove Luau	Best all-around luau	$140 – $230	Ko Olina	Oceanfront, cultural activities, large buffet
Germaine's Luau	Casual, family-friendly	$135 – $195	Kapolei	Beachfront, relaxed atmosphere
Chief's Luau	Most entertaining	$160 – $230	Kapolei	Fun, interactive, comedy-based show
Toa Luau	Most authentic, intimate	$135 – $185	North Shore	Small-group, cultural immersion
Ka Moana Luau	Best oceanfront views	$135 – $195	Honolulu	Stunning views, cultural activities

🌺 Final Tips for Booking a Luau

▪ **Book in advance** – Luaus can sell out, especially during peak seasons.
▪ **Arrive early** – Many luaus offer **pre-show activities** like hula lessons and lei-making.
▪ **Dress comfortably** – Wear **aloha attire or casual resort wear**, and bring a light jacket for cool evenings.
▪ **Pick the right luau for your style** – If you want **high-energy entertainment**,

go for Chief's Luau. If you prefer **a quiet, authentic experience, choose Toa Luau**.

Chapter 8. Culture, History, and Local Experiences

8.1 Polynesian Cultural Center

The **Polynesian Cultural Center (PCC)** is one of the **most immersive cultural experiences in Hawaii**, offering visitors a deep dive into the traditions, history, and daily life of Polynesia. Located in **Laie on Oahu's North Shore**, this **42-acre living museum** features six Polynesian villages, live entertainment, traditional food, and one of the best evening luaus in Hawaii.

📍 Location and Contact Information

- 📍 **Address:** 55-370 Kamehameha Hwy, Laie, HI 96762
- 📞 **Phone:** +1 (808) 293-3333
- 🌐 **Website:** www.polynesia.com
- ⏰ **Hours:** Monday – Saturday, 12:00 PM – 9:00 PM (Closed Sundays)

💲 Ticket Prices & Packages

The PCC offers various ticket options depending on how immersive you want your experience to be:

- 🎟 **General Admission** (Access to villages & cultural exhibits) – **$79.95 (Adult), $63.96 (Child 4-11)**
- 🍽 **Admission + Luau Package** (Includes buffet & evening show) – **$139.95 – $242.95 per person**
- 🌟 **VIP Ambassador Package** (Personalized tour, best seating, exclusive activities) – **$269.95 – $289.95 per person**
- 🎭 **Evening Only Show – "Ha: Breath of Life"** – **$79.95 – $129.95 per person**

👉 **Discounts available for military members, Hawaii residents, and group bookings.**

🌺 Key Attractions & Activities

🏝 Explore Six Polynesian Villages

The PCC features **six villages** representing different Polynesian cultures, each offering interactive activities, performances, and demonstrations.

1. **Hawaiian Village** – Learn hula dancing, try poi pounding, and watch a coconut tree climbing demonstration.
2. **Samoan Village** – Watch Samoan fire-making, coconut husking, and hear traditional drumming.
3. **Tongan Village** – Experience high-energy Tongan drumming shows and audience participation performances.
4. **Fijian Village** – Learn about kava ceremonies and explore authentic Fijian architecture.
5. **Tahiti Village** – Enjoy traditional Tahitian dance and storytelling.
6. **Aotearoa (New Zealand) Village** – Witness the Maori haka (war dance) and explore traditional carvings.

🌊 Canoe Pageant: "Rainbows of Paradise"

⏰ **Time:** 2:30 PM – 3:00 PM

🛶 Experience a **colorful canoe pageant** where performers showcase **traditional dances on floating canoes**, representing the cultures of **Hawaii, Samoa, Tonga, Fiji, Tahiti, and Aotearoa**.

🔥 **"Ha: Breath of Life" – The Night Show**

⏰ **Time:** 7:30 PM – 9:00 PM

🎭 This **breathtaking evening performance** tells a **compelling Polynesian story** through hula, fire dancing, and music. The **fire knife dancers are the highlight** of the show, making it one of Oahu's most exciting cultural experiences.

🍽 **Ali'i Luau – Traditional Hawaiian Feast**

⏰ **Time:** 5:00 PM – 6:30 PM

Indulge in an **authentic Hawaiian luau buffet** featuring:
- 🐖 **Kalua Pig** – Roasted in an imu (underground oven)
- 🍍 **Poke** – Fresh, marinated raw fish
- 🌿 **Poi** – Traditional Hawaiian taro paste
- 🥥 **Haupia** – Coconut pudding

👉 **This is one of the most highly-rated luaus in Oahu**, offering not just a meal but an immersive cultural experience.

🎟 **Visitor Services & Amenities**

✔ **Shuttle Service from Waikiki** (Round-trip transportation available for an additional fee)
✔ **Dining Options** – Luaus, buffet, and food carts with Polynesian cuisine
✔ **Gift Shops** – Souvenirs, handcrafted goods, and Polynesian cultural items
✔ **Photography & Video Services** – Capture your memories with professional photos
✔ **Wheelchair Accessibility** – Fully accessible pathways and seating

🌺 **Why Visit the Polynesian Cultural Center?**

▪ **Most immersive cultural experience in Hawaii**
▪ **Fun for all ages** – Great for families, history lovers, and adventure seekers
▪ **Authentic Polynesian performances, food, and interactive activities**
▪ **"Ha: Breath of Life" – One of the best live shows in Hawaii**

8.2 Bishop Museum

The **Bishop Museum** is the premier museum in Hawaii dedicated to **preserving and showcasing Polynesian and Hawaiian history, culture, and science**. Founded in **1889** by Charles Reed Bishop in honor of his late wife, Princess Bernice Pauahi Bishop, the museum houses the **largest collection of Hawaiian and Pacific artifacts in the world**, making it a must-visit for anyone interested in Hawaii's deep cultural roots and scientific discoveries.

📍 Location and Contact Information

📍 **Address:** 1525 Bernice St, Honolulu, HI 96817
📞 **Phone:** +1 (808) 847-3511
🌐 **Website:** www.bishopmuseum.org
⏰ **Hours:** Open Daily, 9:00 AM – 5:00 PM (Closed on Thanksgiving and Christmas)

💲 Admission Prices

🎟️ **General Admission:**

- Adults (18+) – $28.95
- Seniors (65+) – $25.95
- Youth (4-17) – $19.95
- Children (3 and under) – FREE

👉 Hawaii residents and military members receive discounted rates with valid ID.

🏛️ Key Attractions & Exhibits

🗿 Hawaiian Hall

🗿 This **three-story exhibit** is the heart of the museum, showcasing:

- Ancient **Hawaiian artifacts**, including **royal capes, weapons, and tools**
- A **full-scale model of a traditional Hawaiian canoe**
- Legends and stories of **Hawaiian gods and ali'i (royalty)**

🌐 Pacific Hall

⛵ Explores **Polynesian migration and navigation**, featuring:

- A life-sized **double-hulled voyaging canoe**

- **Maps and models** showing how early Polynesians used the stars to navigate
- Artifacts from **Samoa, Tonga, Fiji, Tahiti, and Aotearoa (New Zealand)**

🔭 J. Watumull Planetarium

One of the best **stargazing and astronomy experiences** in Hawaii!

- **Daily planetarium shows** on Polynesian celestial navigation
- **Interactive exhibits on the Hawaiian night sky**
- **Family-friendly programs** on astronomy and space exploration

🌋 Richard T. Mamiya Science Adventure Center

A fun, hands-on **science exhibit** for all ages featuring:

- A **massive walk-in volcano exhibit** that **simulates an eruption**
- **Interactive displays** about Hawaii's ecosystems and marine life
- **Dinosaur fossils and a deep-sea exploration zone**

🌿 Native Hawaiian Garden

Stroll through a lush garden filled with:

- **Endemic Hawaiian plants** used in traditional medicine and food
- A recreated **lo'i kalo (taro patch)**
- **Guided tours** explaining the significance of different plants

Visitor Services & Amenities

✔️ **Guided Tours** – Available daily, led by expert curators
✔️ **On-Site Café** – Serving Hawaiian-style snacks and drinks
✔️ **Gift Shop** – Hawaiian books, handcrafted jewelry, and cultural souvenirs
✔️ **Wheelchair Accessibility** – Elevators and ramps throughout the museum
✔️ **Parking Available** – Free for museum visitors

🌟 Why Visit the Bishop Museum?

Largest collection of Hawaiian and Pacific artifacts in the world
Perfect for history lovers, families, and science enthusiasts
Engaging exhibits, from Polynesian navigation to erupting volcanoes
J. Watumull Planetarium – A must-visit for astronomy fans

8.3 Historic Downtown Honolulu

Historic Downtown Honolulu is the cultural and political heart of Hawaii, home to some of the most significant **historical landmarks, government buildings, and architectural gems** on the island. This area tells the story of Hawaii's transformation from a **Polynesian kingdom to a U.S. state**, offering visitors a glimpse into its **royal past, colonial influence, and modern governance**.

📍 Location and Contact Information

📍 **Address:** Downtown Honolulu, Honolulu, HI 96813
📞 **Contact:** Varies by attraction (see below)
🌐 **Website:** www.gohawaii.com
⏰ **Hours:** Open year-round, individual sites have specific operating hours

🏛 Key Historic Landmarks & Attractions

👑 Iolani Palace

📍 **Address:** 364 S King St, Honolulu, HI 96813
⏰ **Hours:** Tuesday–Saturday, 9:00 AM – 4:00 PM
💲 **Admission:** $25 (Adults), $10 (Children 5-12)
🌐 **Website:** www.iolanipalace.org
- The **only royal palace in the U.S.**, once home to King Kalakaua and Queen Liliʻuokalani
- Stunning **Hawaiian Renaissance architecture** and original furnishings
- Guided tours available, showcasing **royal artifacts and historical events**

🏛 Hawaii State Capitol

📍 **Address:** 415 S Beretania St, Honolulu, HI 96813
⏰ **Hours:** Monday–Friday, 7:30 AM – 4:30 PM
💲 **Admission:** Free
🌐 **Website:** capitol.hawaii.gov
- Opened in **1969**, designed to reflect Hawaii's natural landscape
- **Columns represent palm trees, reflecting pools symbolize the ocean**
- Visitors can observe **legislative sessions and government proceedings**

🏛 Kawaiaha'o Church

📍 **Address:** 957 Punchbowl St, Honolulu, HI 96813
⏰ **Hours:** Monday–Friday, 8:00 AM – 4:00 PM
💲 **Admission:** Free (Donations appreciated)
🌐 **Website:** www.kawaiahao.org
- One of the **oldest Christian churches** in Hawaii, completed in **1842**
- Made from **coral blocks cut from reefs**, giving it a unique appearance
- Often called the **"Westminster Abbey of the Pacific"** due to its royal connections

⚖️ Ali'iōlani Hale & King Kamehameha Statue

📍 **Address:** 417 S King St, Honolulu, HI 96813
⏰ **Hours:** Monday–Friday, 7:45 AM – 4:30 PM
💲 **Admission:** Free
🌐 **Website:** historichawaii.org
- Houses the **Hawaii State Supreme Court** and judicial offices
- Famous for the **gold-leaf statue of King Kamehameha I**, Hawaii's first ruler
- Featured in many TV shows, including **Hawaii Five-0**

🏛 Mission Houses Museum

📍 **Address:** 553 S King St, Honolulu, HI 96813
⏰ **Hours:** Tuesday–Saturday, 10:00 AM – 4:00 PM
💲 **Admission:** $12 (Adults), $6 (Students & Children)
🌐 **Website:** www.missionhouses.org
- The **oldest standing Western-style buildings** in Hawaii
- Showcases **early missionary life, education, and printing press history**
- Guided tours available, with **historical artifacts and period furniture**

🏙 Things to Do in Historic Downtown Honolulu

🚶 Explore Chinatown

- Discover **local markets, trendy cafés, and historic temples**
- Try **delicious dim sum, poke bowls, and fresh seafood**
- Visit the **Hawaii Theatre**, a restored 1922 venue with live performances

🎨 Visit the Hawaii State Art Museum

- Free entry, showcasing **Hawaiian contemporary art**
- Features **local artists, sculptures, and cultural exhibits**

🚶 Take a Walking Tour

- Self-guided and guided tours available through **Historic Hawaii Foundation**
- See **colonial-era buildings, royal landmarks, and iconic architecture**

■ Visitor Services & Amenities

✔ **Parking:** Paid parking garages and metered street parking available
✔ **Public Transportation:** Easily accessible by **TheBus and Waikiki Trolley**
✔ **Restrooms & Visitor Centers:** Available near major attractions
✔ **Dining & Cafés:** Many local restaurants and food trucks nearby

🌟 Summary: Why Visit Historic Downtown Honolulu?

- Rich in Hawaiian royal history and American colonial influence
- Home to Iolani Palace, the only royal palace in the U.S.
- Architectural beauty blending Polynesian, Asian, and Western styles
- Easy to explore on foot, with historic landmarks close together
- Great for history lovers, culture enthusiasts, and photographers

Chapter 9. Shopping and Nightlife in Oahu

9.1 Best Shopping Areas: Ala Moana Center, Waikiki, Local Boutiques

Oahu is a **shopper's paradise**, offering everything from **luxury brands and designer boutiques to unique Hawaiian souvenirs and locally crafted goods**. Whether you want to **browse high-end fashion, explore outdoor markets, or pick up authentic Hawaiian art and jewelry**, Oahu has shopping spots for every style and budget.

📍 Locations, Hours, and Key Information

Shopping Area	Location	Hours	Website
Ala Moana Center	Honolulu	10 AM – 8 PM (Varies)	www.alamoanacenter.com
Waikiki Shopping District	Waikiki	Varies by store	-
Royal Hawaiian Center	Waikiki	11 AM – 8 PM	www.royalhawaiiancenter.com
Kahala Mall	East Honolulu	10 AM – 8 PM	www.kahalamallcenter.com
Aloha Stadium Swap Meet	Near Pearl Harbor	Wed, Sat, Sun: 8 AM – 3 PM	www.alohastadiumswapmeet.net
Chinatown Markets	Downtown Honolulu	Varies by shop	-

🛍️ Top Shopping Destinations in Oahu

🛒 Ala Moana Center (Honolulu)

📍 **Location:** 1450 Ala Moana Blvd, Honolulu, HI
💲 **Price Range:** $$$ – $$$$
- The **largest open-air shopping mall in the world** with over **350 stores**
- Features **high-end brands** like Gucci, Prada, Louis Vuitton, Chanel
- **Mid-range stores** include Zara, Uniqlo, Lululemon, and Apple
- **Dining options**: Over 100 restaurants and a large food court with **Hawaiian,**

Japanese, and international cuisine
- Offers **live hula performances and cultural activities**

🪧 Waikiki Shopping District

- 📍 **Location:** Kalakaua Avenue, Waikiki
- 💲 **Price Range:** $$ – $$$$
- Iconic shopping street **steps from Waikiki Beach**
- Features luxury stores like **Cartier, Rolex, Tiffany & Co.**
- Many **Hawaiian souvenir shops** selling **handmade jewelry, ukuleles, aloha shirts, and art**
- Home to **popular surf shops** like Quiksilver, Billabong, and Rip Curl
- **Night markets and street vendors** in the evening

👑 Royal Hawaiian Center (Waikiki)

- 📍 **Location:** 2201 Kalakaua Ave, Honolulu, HI
- 💲 **Price Range:** $$$ – $$$$
- Upscale shopping center with **three blocks of high-end boutiques**
- Offers **luxury brands like Fendi, Hermes, and Valentino**
- Hosts **free cultural workshops** like hula lessons and lei-making
- Features **several fine-dining restaurants and cafés**

🏬 Kahala Mall (East Honolulu)

- 📍 **Location:** 4211 Waialae Ave, Honolulu, HI
- 💲 **Price Range:** $$ – $$$
- A **less crowded alternative to Waikiki and Ala Moana**
- Features stores like **Whole Foods, Macy's, and Apple**
- Home to **Hawaiian-owned boutiques selling unique fashion and jewelry**

🎪 Aloha Stadium Swap Meet (Near Pearl Harbor)

- 📍 **Location:** 99-500 Salt Lake Blvd, Honolulu, HI
- 💲 **Price Range:** $ – $$
- **Best place for budget-friendly souvenirs** and handmade goods
- Over **400 vendors selling clothing, art, snacks, and gifts**
- Haggling is **welcome** and often expected
- Great spot to buy **Hawaiian snacks, macadamia nuts, and local crafts**

🍡 Chinatown Markets (Downtown Honolulu)

📍 **Location:** Near Nuuanu Ave & Maunakea St, Honolulu, HI
💲 **Price Range:** $ – $$
- A **historic district** with **fresh produce, seafood, and Asian delicacies**
- Features **local artisan shops and Chinese herbal medicine stores**
- Home to **art galleries, bars, and restaurants**

✨ Summary: Why Shop in Oahu?

■ Luxury shopping, surf brands, and Hawaiian souvenirs all in one place
■ Local markets offer authentic Hawaiian crafts and unique finds
■ Shopping areas often feature live performances, hula shows, and dining
■ A mix of indoor malls, outdoor shopping streets, and night markets

9.2 Oahu's Nightlife: Beachfront Bars, Clubs, and Live Music Venues

Oahu's nightlife is **as vibrant as its beaches**, offering everything from **chic rooftop bars with ocean views** to **energetic clubs, beachside lounges, and live music venues**. Whether you're looking to **sip tropical cocktails under the stars, dance to live DJs, or enjoy an intimate Hawaiian music performance**, Oahu has something for everyone.

🌴 Top Nightlife Spots in Oahu

Venue	Location	Hours	Cover Charge	Website
Sky Waikiki	Waikiki	5 PM – 12 AM	Free – $$	www.skywaikiki.com
Duke's Waikiki	Waikiki Beach	11 AM – 12 AM	Free	www.dukeswaikiki.com

RumFire	Sheraton Waikiki	3 PM – 12 AM	Free	www.rumfirewaikiki.com
The Study at The Modern	Honolulu	6 PM – 12 AM	Free	www.themodernhonolulu.com
Mai Tai Bar	Ala Moana	11 AM – 12 AM	Free	www.maitaibar.com
The Republik	Honolulu	7 PM – 2 AM (Varies)	$$	www.jointherepublik.com

🍹 Beachfront Bars & Lounges

🌆 Sky Waikiki Rooftop Bar

- **Location:** 2270 Kalakaua Ave, Honolulu, HI
- **Price Range:** $$$
- **Stylish rooftop bar with panoramic ocean views**
- Signature cocktails, light bites, and **live DJs**
- **Dress code**: Smart casual

🌴 Duke's Waikiki

- **Location:** 2335 Kalakaua Ave, Honolulu, HI
- **Price Range:** $$
- **Iconic beachfront bar with live Hawaiian music**
- Famous for its **Mai Tais and Hula Pie dessert**
- **Relaxed vibe, great for sunset cocktails**

🔥 RumFire Waikiki

- **Location:** Sheraton Waikiki, Honolulu, HI
- **Price Range:** $$$
- **Trendy bar with fire pits and ocean views**
- Signature **tropical cocktails and tapas**
- **Live DJs on weekends**

🎷 The Study at The Modern

- 📍 **Location:** 1775 Ala Moana Blvd, Honolulu, HI
- 💲 **Price Range:** $$$
- ◆ **Speakeasy-style bar with craft cocktails and jazz music**
- ◆ **Hidden behind a bookshelf**—great for a laid-back evening

💃 Nightclubs & Dance Venues

🎶 The Republik

- 📍 **Location:** 1349 Kapiolani Blvd, Honolulu, HI
- 💲 **Cover Charge:** Varies ($10 – $40)
- ◆ **Best live music venue on Oahu**, hosting local & international artists
- ◆ **Hip-hop, reggae, EDM, and rock concerts**

🔥 Scarlet Honolulu

- 📍 **Location:** 80 S Pauahi St, Honolulu, HI
- 💲 **Cover Charge:** $10 – $20
- ◆ **Hawaii's premier LGBTQ+ nightclub**
- ◆ Features **drag shows, themed parties, and EDM nights**

💃 The District Nightclub

- 📍 **Location:** 1349 Kapiolani Blvd, Honolulu, HI
- 💲 **Cover Charge:** $15+
- ◆ **High-energy nightclub with top DJs and bottle service**
- ◆ Plays **EDM, hip-hop, and top 40 hits**

🎷 Live Music & Hawaiian Entertainment

🎤 Blue Note Hawaii

- 📍 **Location:** Outrigger Waikiki Beach Resort
- 💲 **Cover Charge:** $20 – $50
- ◆ **Premier jazz and live music venue in Honolulu**
- ◆ Features **local and international artists, comedy nights**

🏠 House Without a Key

- 📍 **Location:** Halekulani Hotel, Waikiki
- 💲 **Cover Charge:** Free (food/drink purchase required)

- **Classic Hawaiian music & hula performances**
- Perfect for a romantic evening with ocean views

🎶 **Mai Tai Bar (Ala Moana Center)**

📍 **Location:** 1450 Ala Moana Blvd, Honolulu, HI
💲 **Cover Charge:** Free
- **Casual open-air bar with live music daily**
- Signature **Mai Tais and happy hour specials**

✨ **Summary: Why Experience Oahu's Nightlife?**

◼ Beachfront bars with spectacular sunset views
◼ Live music venues with jazz, Hawaiian, and rock performances
◼ Trendy rooftop lounges and nightclubs with world-class DJs
◼ Local favorites offering traditional Hawaiian entertainment

9.3 Best Spots for Traditional Hawaiian Souvenirs

Bringing home a piece of Oahu is a **must for any traveler**, whether it's **handcrafted jewelry, locally made food products, Hawaiian quilts, or authentic Aloha shirts**. Oahu offers a variety of souvenir shopping experiences, from **bustling**

markets to **high-end boutiques specializing in locally crafted goods**. Here's where to find the **best traditional Hawaiian souvenirs**.

🌴 Best Places to Shop for Traditional Hawaiian Souvenirs

Location	Address	Opening Hours	Best For	Website
Aloha Stadium Swap Meet	99-500 Salt Lake Blvd, Honolulu	Wed, Sat, Sun: 8 AM – 3 PM	Affordable souvenirs, handicrafts	www.alohastadiumswapmeet.net
Hilo Hattie	700 N Nimitz Hwy, Honolulu	10 AM – 6 PM daily	Aloha shirts, macadamia nuts	www.hilohattie.com
Na Mea Hawai'i	1200 Ala Moana Blvd, Honolulu	11 AM – 6 PM daily	Hawaiian books, crafts	www.nameahawaii.com
Honolulu Cookie Company	Multiple locations	10 AM – 9 PM daily	Premium shortbread cookies	www.honolulucookie.com
Polynesian Cultural Center Marketplace	55-370 Kamehameha Hwy, Laie	12 PM – 7 PM (Mon-Sat)	Traditional Hawaiian crafts, ukuleles	www.polynesia.com
Royal Hawaiian Center	2201 Kalakaua Ave, Waikiki	10 AM – 9 PM daily	Upscale Hawaiian souvenirs	www.royalhawaiiancenter.com

🌺 Best Traditional Hawaiian Souvenirs to Buy

🌴 Aloha Shirts & Muumuus

■ **Where to Buy:** Hilo Hattie, Reyn Spooner, Bailey's Antiques & Aloha Shirts
■ **Why Buy It?** A Hawaiian wardrobe staple, these **colorful, floral-patterned shirts and dresses** are perfect for casual wear or a Hawaiian-themed event.

🪵 Handcrafted Koa Wood Products

■ **Where to Buy:** Martin & MacArthur (Ala Moana Center), Polynesian Cultural Center
■ **Why Buy It?** Koa wood is a **rare, native Hawaiian hardwood** used to make **jewelry, pens, bowls, and even ukuleles**.

🌙 Hawaiian Jewelry (Honus, Plumeria, and Puka Shells)

■ **Where to Buy:** Na Hoku, Maui Divers Jewelry, Island Jewelry Waikiki
■ **Why Buy It?** These **delicate pieces feature symbols of Hawaiian culture** like the **honus (sea turtles), plumeria flowers, and puka shells**.

🌺 Hawaiian Quilts

■ **Where to Buy:** Hawaiian Quilt Collection, Na Mea Hawai'i
■ **Why Buy It?** Handmade Hawaiian quilts feature **unique island-inspired patterns** and make for **beautiful heirloom gifts**.

🎵 Ukuleles

■ **Where to Buy:** The Ukulele Store (Royal Hawaiian Center), Kamaka Ukulele
■ **Why Buy It?** A great **musical souvenir**, available in **affordable tourist versions or professional-quality handcrafted pieces**.

● Hawaiian Food Products

■ **Where to Buy:** Honolulu Cookie Company, Big Island Candies, ABC Stores
■ **Why Buy It? Macadamia nuts, Kona coffee, pineapple wine, and Hawaiian shortbread cookies** make excellent edible souvenirs.

🛍 Top Shopping Spots for Authentic Souvenirs

🛒 Aloha Stadium Swap Meet

- **Location:** 99-500 Salt Lake Blvd, Honolulu
- **Price Range:** $ – Affordable
- **Hawaii's largest open-air market** with over **400 vendors**
- Best place for **budget-friendly souvenirs, Hawaiian shirts, and crafts**
- **Cash preferred**, but some vendors accept credit cards

🌺 Hilo Hattie

- **Location:** 700 N Nimitz Hwy, Honolulu
- **Price Range:** $$ – Moderate
- Famous for **Aloha shirts, macadamia nut chocolates, and souvenirs**
- Offers **free samples of Kona coffee and chocolates**

📖 Na Mea Hawai'i

- **Location:** 1200 Ala Moana Blvd, Honolulu
- **Price Range:** $$ – Moderate
- Specializes in **Hawaiian books, music, crafts, and locally made gifts**
- Great for **cultural souvenirs and one-of-a-kind artisan pieces**

🍍 Polynesian Cultural Center Marketplace

- **Location:** 55-370 Kamehameha Hwy, Laie
- **Price Range:** $$ – Moderate
- Offers **handmade Polynesian crafts, ukuleles, and artwork**
- **Great place for cultural souvenirs** after visiting the **PCC's live shows**

👜 Royal Hawaiian Center

- **Location:** 2201 Kalakaua Ave, Waikiki
- **Price Range:** $$$ – High-end
- Upscale shopping with **Hawaiian-inspired luxury brands**
- Home to **high-end Hawaiian jewelry and fashion boutiques**

✨ Summary: Where to Find the Best Hawaiian Souvenirs?

■ **For Budget-Friendly Souvenirs:** Aloha Stadium Swap Meet
■ **For High-Quality Aloha Wear:** Hilo Hattie, Reyn Spooner
■ **For Traditional Handcrafted Gifts:** Na Mea Hawai'i, Polynesian Cultural Center

- **For Hawaiian Jewelry & Koa Wood Gifts:** Martin & MacArthur, Na Hoku
- **For Edible Hawaiian Treats:** Honolulu Cookie Company, ABC Stores

Chapter 10. Appendices

10.1 Packing Checklist for Oahu

Packing for a trip to Oahu requires a balance of **beach essentials, outdoor gear, and casual island attire**. Whether you're **relaxing on Waikiki Beach, hiking Diamond Head, or exploring historic sites**, this checklist ensures you're well-prepared.

🌴 Essentials for Every Traveler

- ◼ **Valid ID or Passport** – Required for flights and hotel check-ins.
- ◼ **Credit Cards & Cash** – Most places accept cards, but small vendors may prefer cash.
- ◼ **Travel Insurance** – Covers unexpected cancellations, medical emergencies, and trip disruptions.
- ◼ **Phone & Charger** – Consider a waterproof phone case for beach days.
- ◼ **Printed Copies of Reservations** – Hotel, rental car, excursions, and important

contacts.

👕 Clothing & Footwear

For the Beach & Water Activities:
- **Swimsuits** – Bring at least **two** for easy rotation.
- **Beach Cover-Up / Rash Guard** – Sun protection and comfort after swimming.
- **Flip-Flops / Sandals** – Waterproof and easy to slip on/off.
- **Quick-Dry Towel** – Compact and perfect for beach outings.

For Exploring & Sightseeing:
- **Lightweight T-Shirts & Tank Tops** – Breathable for warm, humid weather.
- **Casual Shorts & Skirts** – Comfortable and easy to mix & match.
- **Sundress / Aloha Shirt** – Stylish yet relaxed for luaus or dining out.
- **Light Sweater or Jacket** – Evenings can be cooler, especially in winter.
- **Comfortable Walking Shoes** – Sneakers or hiking shoes for long walks.
- **Water Shoes** – Essential for snorkeling at rocky beaches like Shark's Cove.

For Hiking & Outdoor Adventures:
- **Moisture-Wicking Shirt** – Keeps you cool and dry.
- **Leggings or Athletic Shorts** – Comfortable for active excursions.
- **Hat & Sunglasses** – Protects against the strong Hawaiian sun.
- **Rain Jacket or Poncho** – Sudden showers are common, especially in winter.

🛍️ Beach & Outdoor Essentials

- **Reef-Safe Sunscreen** (*Hawaii bans sunscreens with oxybenzone and octinoxate*).
- **Aloe Vera Gel** – Helps soothe sunburns.
- **Bug Spray** – Especially useful for hikes in tropical areas.
- **Reusable Water Bottle** – Stay hydrated while reducing plastic waste.
- **Snorkel Gear** – Many beaches have rental shops, but bringing your own ensures quality.
- **Dry Bag** – Protects electronics and valuables during beach or boat trips.
- **Underwater Camera / GoPro** – Capture stunning marine life and waterfalls.

🧴 Health & Toiletries

- **Prescribed Medications** – Bring enough for your trip duration.
- **Motion Sickness Bands or Pills** – Useful for boat tours or winding mountain roads.
- **Lip Balm with SPF** – The sun and ocean breeze can dry out lips quickly.
- **Hand Sanitizer & Wet Wipes** – Useful for public transport and outdoor

excursions.

■ **First Aid Kit** – Band-aids, antiseptic wipes, pain relievers, and allergy meds.

🎒 Gadgets & Extras

■ **Portable Power Bank** – For charging phones on the go.
■ **Travel Adapter** – U.S. uses **Type A/B plugs** (110V).
■ **Small Backpack or Daypack** – Ideal for hikes and city exploration.
■ **Book or Kindle** – Perfect for relaxing on the beach.
■ **Journal / Travel Notebook** – Great for documenting your experiences.

🏝 Special Packing Tips by Season

☀ Summer (June – August):
- Pack **extra sun protection** – hats, sunglasses, and a **cooling towel**.
- Light **breathable fabrics** are key for hot and humid days.

❄ Winter (December – February):
- Bring **a light sweater or windbreaker** for cooler evenings.
- A **rain jacket** is recommended for wetter months.

🌿 Spring & Fall:
- Weather is mild, but **light rain gear** may be helpful.
- **Pack layers** for unpredictable temperatures.

✈ What Not to Pack

🚫 **Non-Reef-Safe Sunscreen** – Hawaii bans sunscreens with harmful chemicals.
🚫 **Too Many Fancy Outfits** – Hawaii is **casual**; even upscale restaurants accept Aloha attire.
🚫 **Heavy Coats & Boots** – Even in winter, the coldest it gets is around 65°F (18°C).
🚫 **Plastic Bags & Styrofoam Containers** – Banned in Hawaii to protect the environment

🌺 Final Packing Advice

Oahu's **laid-back island vibe** means you **don't need to overpack**. Essentials like **sunscreen, hats, and beach towels** are easy to find locally. Bring **versatile outfits, adventure gear, and reef-safe products**, and you'll be all set for an amazing trip!

10.2 Essential Travel Tips and Local Etiquette

Visiting Oahu is an unforgettable experience, but understanding local customs, etiquette, and travel tips will ensure you have a smooth and respectful visit. Hawaiians deeply value their culture, land, and traditions, so following these guidelines will help you blend in and show respect to the locals.

🌺 Cultural Etiquette & Respecting Hawaiian Traditions

■ **Respect 'Āina (The Land)** – Hawaiians have a strong connection to nature. Do not disturb sacred sites, remove rocks or sand, or step on coral reefs.

■ **Honor Sacred Places** – Sites like **Iolani Palace, Heiau (ancient Hawaiian temples), and Pearl Harbor** are of great cultural and historical importance. Act respectfully, keep noise levels low, and follow any posted guidelines.

■ **Use "Aloha" & "Mahalo"** – "Aloha" means hello, goodbye, and love, while "Mahalo" means thank you. Using these words is appreciated by locals.

■ **Don't Touch or Disturb Wildlife** – **Sea turtles (honu) and monk seals** are protected under law. Keep a **10-foot** distance and admire from afar. Feeding fish or chasing marine life while snorkeling is discouraged.

■ **Remove Your Shoes Indoors** – Many Hawaiian homes and even some businesses prefer you remove your shoes before entering. Look for a pile of shoes by the door as a cue.

■ **Accept a Lei with Grace** – If someone gives you a **lei (flower necklace)**, always accept it with appreciation. It is disrespectful to refuse or remove a lei in front of the giver.

■ **Respect the Spirit of Aloha** – Hawaiians value kindness, patience, and hospitality. A laid-back, friendly attitude will make your experience more enjoyable.

🚗 Transportation & Getting Around Oahu

■ **Rent a Car for Flexibility** – While Oahu has public transportation, renting a car gives you more freedom, especially for North Shore and East Oahu exploration.

■ **Use "The Bus" for Budget Travel** – Oahu's public bus system is affordable ($3 per ride or $7.50 for a day pass). It covers most tourist areas, but routes to remote beaches and hiking spots can be limited.

■ **Expect Heavy Traffic in Honolulu** – Rush hour (7-9 AM & 3-6 PM) can be slow, so plan accordingly. Use navigation apps to check real-time conditions.

■ **Parking Can Be Expensive** – Waikiki hotels charge around **$30-$50 per night** for parking. Look for free or metered parking in nearby areas to save money.

■ **Drive with Aloha** – Locals drive courteously. Avoid honking unless necessary, and **let people merge** when possible. Be mindful of pedestrians and cyclists.

🌊 **Beach & Ocean Safety Tips**

■ **Check Ocean Conditions** – Currents can be strong, especially in winter. Look for **posted signs and lifeguard warnings** before swimming.

■ **Follow Surf Etiquette** – If surfing, respect the **local hierarchy** in the lineup. Don't drop in on another surfer's wave.

■ **Protect Coral Reefs** – Use **reef-safe sunscreen** and **avoid stepping on coral** while snorkeling. Coral is fragile and takes years to grow back.

■ **Beware of Strong Currents** – North Shore beaches like **Waimea Bay and Sunset Beach** can have powerful waves, especially in winter. Stick to lifeguarded beaches if unsure.

■ **Watch for Box Jellyfish** – These can appear **8-10 days after a full moon**. Check local beach reports and bring **vinegar** to neutralize stings if needed.

■ **Stay Hydrated & Use Sun Protection** – The Hawaiian sun is strong. Wear a **hat, sunglasses, and SPF 30+ sunscreen**, and drink plenty of water.

🍍 **Dining & Food Etiquette**

■ **Try Local Foods** – Sample **poke, laulau, loco moco, malasadas, and shave ice** to experience authentic Hawaiian flavors.

■ **Tip Accordingly** – Tipping is expected in Hawaii:

- **Restaurants** – 15-20%
- **Bars** – $1-$2 per drink
- **Tour Guides** – $5-$10 per person for group tours, more for private guides

■ **Make Reservations for Popular Restaurants** – High-demand spots like **Duke's Waikiki and Mama's Fish House** (on Maui) book up weeks in advance.

■ **Respect "Island Time"** – Service may be slower than on the mainland. Relax and enjoy the laid-back pace.

■ **Support Local Farmers' Markets & Food Trucks** – They offer fresh, local produce and affordable, delicious meals.

🛍 Shopping & Souvenirs

■ **Buy Authentic Hawaiian Souvenirs** – Skip mass-produced trinkets and look for **local crafts, Hawaiian quilts, koa wood carvings, and ukuleles**.

■ **Avoid Purchasing Coral & Lava Rocks** – Taking lava rocks from Hawaii is considered bad luck according to local legends.

■ **Shop at Local Businesses** – Support Hawaiian artisans by purchasing from small boutiques and craft fairs rather than big chains.

🌿 Responsible & Sustainable Travel Tips

■ **Reduce Plastic Waste** – Hawaii has strict **plastic bans**, so bring a **reusable water bottle, tote bags, and metal straws**.

■ **Use Eco-Friendly Sunscreen** – Protect marine life by choosing **reef-safe** sunscreen without oxybenzone or octinoxate.

■ **Stay on Marked Trails** – Avoid damaging ecosystems by **not veering off hiking paths**.

■ **Respect Local Wildlife** – Don't feed wild animals or disturb natural habitats.

■ **Limit Single-Use Items** – Many places **don't offer plastic bags**, so bring a reusable tote for shopping.

■ **Volunteer Opportunities** – If interested, consider giving back by joining a **beach cleanup** or local conservation effort.

📍 Final Travel Tips for Oahu

- **Book Activities in Advance** – Popular tours, luaus, and excursions sell out fast. Reserve early to secure spots.
- **Carry Cash for Small Vendors** – Farmers' markets, food trucks, and local shops may prefer cash.
- **Respect Local Communities** – Avoid loud music, littering, and trespassing on private property.

- **Be Flexible & Embrace Aloha Spirit** – Things may not always go as planned, but a positive attitude will make your trip memorable.

🌺 Summary: Embracing the Aloha Spirit

Oahu is more than just a beautiful island—it is a place with a **rich history, deep cultural traditions, and a strong sense of community**. By being **mindful of Hawaiian customs, respecting the land, and practicing sustainable travel**, you can fully embrace the **spirit of Aloha** and make the most of your visit to paradise.

10.3 Emergency Contacts and Health Services in Oahu

When traveling to Oahu, it's essential to be prepared for emergencies. Here's a list of important contacts, hospitals, and health services to ensure you stay safe and get the help you need when necessary.

📞 Emergency Phone Numbers

- **General Emergency (Police, Fire, Medical)** – **911** (Available 24/7)
- **Non-Emergency Police Assistance** – (808) 529-3111
- **Hawaiʻi Poison Control Center** – 1-800-222-1222
- **Hawaiʻi Department of Health** – (808) 586-4400
- **Hawaiʻi Tourism Authority Visitor Assistance** – (808) 973-2255
- **U.S. Coast Guard Search & Rescue** – (808) 535-3333

🏥 Hospitals & Medical Centers

Oahu has several **high-quality hospitals, urgent care clinics, and pharmacies** available for travelers. If you experience a medical emergency, dial **911** or go to the nearest hospital.

Major Hospitals (24/7 Emergency Care)

[1] **The Queen's Medical Center** (Largest Hospital in Hawaii)

- 📍 **Address:** 1301 Punchbowl St, Honolulu, HI 96813
- ☎ **Phone:** (808) 691-1000
- 🌐 **Website:** www.queens.org
- 🏥 **Key Features:** Level I Trauma Center, Stroke & Cardiac Care, 24/7 Emergency Services

2️⃣ **Straub Medical Center**

- 📍 **Address:** 888 S King St, Honolulu, HI 96813
- ☎ **Phone:** (808) 522-4000
- 🌐 **Website:** www.hawaiipacifichealth.org
- 💼 **Key Features:** 24/7 ER, Specialized in Orthopedics & Internal Medicine

3️⃣ **Adventist Health Castle** (Best for Windward Oahu Visitors)

- 📍 **Address:** 640 Ulukahiki St, Kailua, HI 96734
- ☎ **Phone:** (808) 263-5500
- 🌐 **Website:** www.adventisthealth.org/castle
- 💼 **Key Features:** 24/7 ER, Family-Friendly Services, Located Near Kailua & Lanikai

4️⃣ **Kaiser Permanente Moanalua Medical Center** (For Kaiser Members)

- 📍 **Address:** 3288 Moanalua Rd, Honolulu, HI 96819
- ☎ **Phone:** (808) 432-0000
- 🌐 **Website:** www.kaiserpermanente.org
- 💼 **Key Features:** 24/7 ER, Specialized Care for Kaiser Members

💼 **Urgent Care Clinics (Non-Emergency Medical Needs)**

If your condition is not life-threatening, visiting an **urgent care clinic** is a faster and more affordable alternative to a hospital ER.

1️⃣ **Hale Pawa'a Urgent Care**

- 📍 **Address:** 1401 S Beretania St #350, Honolulu, HI 96814
- ☎ **Phone:** (808) 469-4900
- ⏰ **Hours:** Mon-Fri: 8 AM – 8 PM | Sat-Sun: 8 AM – 6 PM

2️⃣ **Urgent Care Hawaii – Waikiki** (Great for Tourists)

- 📍 **Address:** 1860 Ala Moana Blvd #101, Honolulu, HI 96815
- ☎ **Phone:** (808) 456-2273
- 🌐 **Website:** www.ucarehi.com
- ⏰ **Hours:** Daily 8 AM – 8 PM

3️⃣ **Doctors of Waikiki** (24/7 Medical Assistance for Tourists)

- 📍 **Address:** 2155 Kalakaua Ave #308, Honolulu, HI 96815
- 📞 **Phone:** (808) 922-2112
- 🌐 **Website:** www.doctorsofwaikiki.com
- 💼 **Key Features:** Open 24/7, Walk-Ins Welcome, Specializes in Tourist Care

💊 **Pharmacies & Medication Needs**

Most pharmacies are open late, and some operate **24/7** for emergencies.

Major Pharmacy Chains in Oahu

1️⃣ **Longs Drugs (CVS Pharmacy)** – Multiple Locations

- **24/7 Location:** 2155 Kalakaua Ave, Honolulu, HI 96815 (Waikiki)
- 📞 **Phone:** (808) 922-8797

2️⃣ **Walgreens Pharmacy**

- **Location:** 1121 S Beretania St, Honolulu, HI 96814
- ⏰ **Hours:** 6 AM – 12 AM (Midnight)
- 📞 **Phone:** (808) 535-1782

3️⃣ **Walmart Pharmacy** (Budget-Friendly Prescriptions)

- **Location:** 700 Keeaumoku St, Honolulu, HI 96814
- 📞 **Phone:** (808) 955-8441

4️⃣ **Costco Pharmacy** (For Costco Members)

- **Location:** 525 Alakawa St, Honolulu, HI 96817
- 📞 **Phone:** (808) 526-6103

🦟 **Common Travel Health Concerns & Prevention**

🦠 **COVID-19 & Flu** – Stay up to date on vaccinations and carry a **mask & sanitizer** if needed.

☀️ **Sunburn & Heatstroke** – Use SPF 30+ sunscreen, wear a hat, and stay hydrated.

🦟 **Mosquito-Borne Illnesses** – Use insect repellent, especially in rainforest areas like **Manoa Falls**.

🌊 **Swimmer's Ear & Ocean Infections** – Avoid swallowing ocean water and dry ears properly after swimming.

📌 **Final Emergency & Health Travel Tips for Oahu**

✔️ **Know Your Insurance Coverage** – Check if your travel insurance covers medical emergencies in Hawaii.
✔️ **Keep Emergency Contacts Handy** – Save **local hospitals & your country's consulate** in your phone.
✔️ **Carry a Basic First Aid Kit** – Band-aids, motion sickness pills, and pain relievers can be useful.
✔️ **Drink Bottled or Filtered Water** – Tap water is safe, but sensitive stomachs may prefer filtered.
✔️ **Stay Calm & Seek Help Immediately** – Whether it's an accident, illness, or lost passport, act fast and call for assistance.

🌺 **Summary: Staying Safe & Healthy in Oahu**

While Oahu is a paradise, being prepared for emergencies ensures peace of mind. Knowing **where to find hospitals, urgent care clinics, pharmacies, and key emergency contacts** can make all the difference in an unexpected situation.

10.4 Useful Apps and Websites for Travelers in Oahu

Traveling in Oahu is easier with the right apps and websites at your fingertips. From navigating public transportation to finding the best local eats, these resources will help you make the most of your trip.

📍 **Navigation & Transportation Apps**

🚗 **Google Maps** (Android | iOS)

- Best for **driving directions, bus routes, and walking paths**
- Offers **live traffic updates and offline maps**

🚌 **TheBus – DaBus2** (Android | iOS)

- Official app for **Oahu's public bus system**
- Shows **real-time bus arrivals and route planning**

🚖 **Uber / Lyft** (Uber | Lyft)

- Ideal for **quick and convenient rides around Oahu**

- Cheaper than taxis, especially for **Waikiki to North Shore trips**

🚲 **Biki Bikeshare** (Android | iOS)

- Bike rental app for **exploring Honolulu and Waikiki**
- Check **real-time availability and station locations**

✈ **HNL Airport App** (Website)

- Get **real-time flight status updates** for **Daniel K. Inouye International Airport (HNL)**
- Find **baggage claim info, parking, and terminal maps**

🌊 **Outdoor Activities & Adventure Apps**

🏄 **Surfline** (Android | iOS)

- Live **surf reports and wave forecasts** for Oahu's beaches
- Great for surfers checking **Waikiki, North Shore, and Makaha waves**

🌊 **Hawaii Beach Safety** (Website)

- Real-time updates on **ocean conditions, jellyfish alerts, and high surf warnings**
- Covers **popular beaches like Hanauma Bay, Lanikai, and Sunset Beach**

🌀 **Tides Near Me** (Android | iOS)

- Helps plan **fishing, snorkeling, and tidepool adventures**
- Shows **daily tide charts for Oahu's coastline**

🥾 **AllTrails** (Android | iOS)

- Best for **hiking trail maps, difficulty ratings, and reviews**
- Find **top hikes like Diamond Head, Manoa Falls, and Koko Head**

📡 **Gaia GPS** (Android | iOS)

- Offline **GPS maps for hiking, camping, and exploring**
- Useful for **trails with limited cell service**

🍴 **Food & Dining Apps**

🍴 **Yelp** (Android | iOS)

- Find **top-rated restaurants, bars, and food trucks**
- Read **reviews and see menus before dining**

🚚 **Hawaiian Food Trucks App** (Website)

- Shows **locations of popular food trucks in Oahu**
- Track trucks like **Giovanni's Shrimp, Leonard's Malasadas, and Ono Seafood**

🍍 **OpenTable** (Android | iOS)

- Make **restaurant reservations** at top spots like Duke's Waikiki
- Avoid long wait times, especially for **Luaus and fine dining**

🛍️ **Shopping & Souvenirs**

🛒 **Shop Oahu** (Website)

- Directory of **Ala Moana Center, Waikiki shops, and local boutiques**
- Find **Hawaiian souvenirs, designer brands, and island-made crafts**

🎁 **Made in Hawaii Festival App** (Website)

- Showcases **local artisans, handmade gifts, and island crafts**
- Check for **event dates, vendor lists, and discounts**

🎭 **Culture & History Apps**

🏛️ **Bishop Museum Guide** (Website)

- Learn about **Hawaiian history, Polynesian culture, and interactive exhibits**
- Find **hours, ticket prices, and special events**

🗝️ **Polynesian Cultural Center App** (Website)

- Plan your visit to **Oahu's top cultural attraction**
- Book tickets for **Luau experiences and traditional performances**

📖 **Hawaiian Language & Culture Apps**

- **ʻŌlelo Hawaiʻi** (iOS) – Learn **basic Hawaiian phrases**
- **Duolingo** (Android | iOS) – Hawaiian language lessons

📣 General Travel Apps & Resources

💰 XE Currency Converter (Android | iOS)

- **Convert currencies** and check live exchange rates

🛡 Google Translate (Android | iOS)

- Helps with **language translation**, including Hawaiian phrases

🏨 Expedia / Booking.com (Expedia | Booking)

- Compare prices for **hotels, vacation rentals, and flights**

🌴 GoHawaii (Website)

- Official **Hawaii Tourism website** for travel tips, itineraries, and safety info

🌺 Summary: Your Digital Travel Companion for Oahu

Having the right apps can enhance your **Oahu experience**, whether you need **transportation, food recommendations, or outdoor adventure guides**. Download a few of these before your trip to make exploring **Hawaii's most famous island** stress-free and enjoyable!

10.5 Recommended Reading and Resources

Enhance your Oahu travel experience with these **books, travel guides, documentaries, and websites** that provide deeper insights into the island's history, culture, and must-see attractions. Whether you're looking for an **in-depth historical perspective**, **local travel tips**, or **Hawaiian legends**, these resources will help you appreciate Oahu beyond its stunning beaches and resorts.

Hawaiian History & Culture

- "Shoal of Time: A History of the Hawaiian Islands" – Gavan Daws
    - A **classic book on Hawaii's history**, from **ancient Polynesian settlers to modern times.**
- "Captive Paradise: A History of Hawaii" – James L. Haley
    - A **detailed account of Hawaii's monarchy, American annexation, and statehood.**
- "The Legends and Myths of Hawaii" – David Kalakaua
    - Written by Hawaii's last reigning king, this book explores **ancient Hawaiian mythology and folklore.**

- "Hawaiian Mythology" – Martha Beckwith
  - A deeper look into **Hawaiian gods, spirits, and legendary stories**.

Hawaiian Language & Traditions

- **"ʻŌlelo Noʻeau: Hawaiian Proverbs and Poetical Sayings"** – Mary Kawena Pukui
  - A collection of **traditional Hawaiian proverbs**, offering insight into the **island's wisdom and customs**.
- "The Hawaiian Dictionary" – Mary Kawena Pukui & Samuel H. Elbert
  - Essential for travelers wanting to **learn common Hawaiian words and phrases**.
- **"Hawaiian Blood: Colonialism and the Politics of Sovereignty and Indigeneity"** – J. Kēhaulani Kauanui
  - Discusses the **impact of colonialism on Hawaiian identity and sovereignty movements**.

🎬 Documentaries & Films

Culture & History

- "Hawaiian: The Legend of Eddie Aikau" (2013) – ESPN's 30 for 30
  - A powerful story about **Hawaiian surf legend and lifeguard Eddie Aikau**, who embodied the **spirit of aloha and ocean conservation**.
- **"Act of War: The Overthrow of the Hawaiian Nation" (1993)**
  - A **must-watch** for understanding **Hawaii's annexation and political history**.
- "Hawaiʻi: The Stolen Paradise" (2019)
  - Explores **Hawaii's indigenous culture, tourism impact, and local activism**.

Nature & Conservation

- "Hawaiian Islands: The Pacific Paradise" (BBC Earth)
  - Showcases **Oahu's diverse landscapes, wildlife, and environmental challenges**.
- **"Saving Ohia: The Fight Against Rapid ʻŌhiʻa Death" (PBS Hawaii)**
  - Highlights the **threats to Hawaii's native forests and conservation efforts**.
- "Riding Giants" (2004)
  - A surf documentary featuring **Oahu's North Shore and the evolution of big wave surfing**.

🌐 Websites & Online Resources

Official Tourism & Travel Planning

- GoHawaii.com – Hawaii's official tourism website
- Hawaii.com – Travel tips, deals, and local event listings
- Oahu Visitors Bureau – Insights on **things to do, where to stay, and cultural experiences**

Outdoor Adventure & Safety

- Hawaii Beach Safety – Up-to-date **ocean conditions and safety warnings**
- AllTrails – Reviews and maps for **Oahu's best hiking trails**
- Hawaii State Parks – Info on **state parks, permits, and closures**

Local News & Events

- Honolulu Star-Advertiser – Oahu's **main newspaper** for local news and events
- Hawaii News Now – Weather updates, road closures, and live reports
- Hawaii Public Radio – Cultural stories, local interviews, and Hawaiian music

Hawaiian Language & Culture

- Ulukau Hawaiian Electronic Library – Free **Hawaiian language resources and historical archives**
- Hawaiian Cultural Center – Educational resources on **Hawaiian traditions and heritage**

🎬 Summary: Your Guide to Learning More About Oahu

These documentaries and websites provide **a deeper understanding of Oahu's history, culture, and travel experiences**. Whether you're looking for **practical travel advice, local traditions, or conservation efforts**, these resources will enrich your journey and help you appreciate **Hawaii beyond its stunning scenery**.

Printed in Dunstable, United Kingdom